FORSAKING THE FAMILY

FORSAKING
THE FAMILY

JESUS, CHILDHOOD AND
THE SEARCH FOR FREEDOM

by

SIMON PARKE

Forsaking the Family

Jesus, Childhood and the Search for Freedom

First published in Great Britain in 2005
Copyright © 2011 Simon Parke. All rights reserved.

Published and printed in the United States of America and the United Kingdom
by White Crow Books; an imprint of White Crow Productions Ltd.

For information, contact White Crow Books
at P. O. Box 1013 Guildford, GU1 9EJ United Kingdom,
or e-mail to info@whitecrowbooks.com.

Cover Designed by Butterflyeffect
Interior production by essentialworks.co.uk
Interior design by Perseus Design

Paperback ISBN 978-1-907661-51-8
eBook ISBN 978-1-907661-52-5

Non Fiction / Body, Mind & Spirit / Psychology

Published by White Crow Books
www.whitecrowbooks.com

I dedicate this book to my dear friends,
Chloe and Harry, who must now go free

Contents

Welcome

This is a little book about our experience of family and childhood. The shape of family arrangements varies greatly, of course, and this is one of the reasons for the family's success. It remains the oldest human institution precisely because it is so flexible and fluid, constantly reinventing itself down the centuries, across the world and in our lives, in ever-different forms. We therefore contemplate a subject effortlessly topical, for the family, like the poor, is always with us. It has a long history, an influential present and an assured future.

In all societies, family is a sacred cow, and each generation is offered no alternative other than to get in line and bow to the sacred cow's authority and goodness. But allegiance to any cause should not be offered without due consideration, and so in this book, we will consider a little.

*

Consider yourself, at home;
Consider yourself, one of the family

So goes the cheery song in the musical *Oliver*. But Jesus, it appears, never considered himself one of the family and that may be a surprisingly liberating truth for many. The family is a given but that does not mean it's always a glory. Certainly Jesus' family values had nothing to do with the trite and moralistic nonsense that passes for home truths in contemporary life.

At the age of twelve, Jesus absented himself from his parents to stay talking in the temple with adults in whom he was interested. His parents were understandably distraught by the time they found him, but Jesus saw such worry as their problem and not his. The only misdemeanour he could perceive in the situation was their misguided attempt to control him.

Later in his life, we hear of a brief and uncomfortable incident involving Jesus and his brothers. They appear to have little faith in him, or understand very much about the shape of his heart or aspirations for life. Jesus protects himself by deceiving them about his intentions. In short, he lies to them in order to be rid of them.

He also disowned his mother at one point in his life. He was talking to people in his usual manner, when he got the message that his mother, brothers and sisters were outside waiting to see him. They felt he needed some corrective words, some wise advice. Jesus refused to see them, and instead carried on talking with those he was with. 'Who is my mother anyway?' he asked. 'My mother, brothers and sisters are those who obey God.' Jesus had destroyed the foundations of family life and family values in little under twenty words, spoken in anger at the way things were.

And then toward the end of his life, in a most moving scene, Jesus again plays fast and loose with traditional notions of family, by creating a new one from the cross.

'Mary, here is your son,' he said to his mother, concerning John. 'John, here is your mother,' he said to John concerning Mary. After family, there was family. But then Jesus' closest family member was probably his friend Mary Magdalene.

Jesus did not accept the dominant position of family in his culture. He lived in opposition to it, never bowing to this particular sacred cow. Instead, he looked through it, in search of what was truthful and strong, beyond the restrictive and manipulative institution it had become.

It was a most shocking stance to adopt in the circumstances, and often not a pretty sight, for the holy family as lived by Jesus involved truancy, disdain, anger, deception, and staggering rudeness.

The actions and words of Jesus concerning family would not survive beyond his death, however, amid the moralistic accretions of the passing years and the demands of society and religion. A wall of silence developed around his attitudes and actions and a strong gate erected with a large sign saying 'No Entry'. But we will ignore the sign, push the gate a little and squeeze inside, for there is here a very intriguing and hopeful garden to explore.

*

The great and good love family values; it is a fine sounding phrase and always in season. Family values is sewn on the banner of all politicians, while remaining the insistent lobby of the religious also. It is, however, not only a meaningless phrase but a dangerous one. For families have the capacity to destroy people, being the single most manipulative force in the world today. Most families incorporate a well-organized set of prejudice, false assumption and discreet or blatant mistreatment. For evidence of their effects we need only look at the human race or, more pertinently, ourselves. We each live the damage done by our families, but do we question them? Not often, because it simply isn't allowed.

The sacred cow of family deserves only worship, which leaves the crying child within us, desperate and unheard. The child thus smothered takes its revenge daily.

*

There is in fact no such thing as family. It is a word heavy with association but light on precision. Neither history nor the dictionary affords it a particular meaning or form written in stone. It describes a set of connections to do with parentage, ancestry or household. It describes a wide variety of structures of relating, from a medieval household including lord, lady, legitimate offspring, ladies in waiting, servants, illegitimate offspring, retainers, dogs and grandma, to a lay community of women on a windswept island; from a small flat in London where a white couple live with their two adopted children from Guatemala, to a native American settlement where the family is the tribe.

Family describes connections and structures. It says nothing, however, about the quality of those connections or structures, and in the business of life, it is only the quality of relationship which matters.

If the sacred cow of family is worth anything, it will be because of the quality of relationship created.

*

The unconscious will see no need for this book, for being strangers to themselves, they will be strangers also to the need to discover what created them. They will not wish their sleep-walking disturbed, and will be angry at this unnecessary muck-raking. But for those stirring from sleep; for those glimpsing the possibility of consciousness and beginning to smell the coffee of life in their own particular way - they will be most interested to reflect on the institution which created us all, and in particular, the one which created them.

Life is not complicated. It is difficult, but it is not complicated, for it is about two things and two things only. First, there is the discernment of where life lies for you, and second, there is the choosing of it.

It is simple really: true discernment followed by brave action. We feel our way towards what is life-giving for us in the world, which may take time; and then we consider how it best may be achieved and begin to act on this inner encounter with hope. There can be few arenas in life where these twin callings of discernment and action are more pressing than in the territory of family.

How we relate to our family is a personal business, for no two families are the same and no two people are the same. But it is the contention here that to live in rebellion against them is as foolish as living in their thrall; that ultimately, there is life neither in kicking out nor in obedient collusion. Beyond both states, and both claustrophobic sets of agendas, is something better: freedom of relationship. This is a relating which does not for a moment collude in negativity or manipulation, but, equally, does not sulk or lash out in unhappy tantrum.

Daily, this freedom offers itself anew to the world, for today is all there is: yesterday is done, and tomorrow does not exist. This is a freedom of relating which grows out of a clear sense of our own identity. It is only when we know who we are that we can offer ourselves very merrily to others. It is therefore a freedom which is at once knowingly separate and gladly relating.

And such a state is very good news. It is the freedom of those who have seen through family and discovered another citizenship; the freedom of those who know that their true family is not those caught up in the same little biological tangle as themselves or those with whom they share a household. Rather, their family is the world; a world in which they are at once both distinct from all and united to all.

So welcome now to the original holy family, with whom we will walk a little. Unlike the Christmas birth, they were a long way from stable.

Separation from family

PART ONE

Meet Marie who will lead us into this chapter. She was always daddy's best girl, though she is an adult now and trying to find a man who she can please. Her body is not happy; she doesn't seem to live in it comfortably. It causes her problems mainly because she is so out of touch with it, for all is sacrificed amid the unconscious drive towards a perfect marriage. For this, she will do anything; anything to win the perfect man.

Unfortunately, she is in love with an illusion - an ideal which doesn't exist. Daddy's best girl is searching for an idealized projection of her father. Do not criticize her. But rather, give her gentle space to weep and sob for the one she left behind: the dear child she abandoned - her small self - when she first set out to do the right thing, and please daddy.

Daddy is dead now, but that is strangely irrelevant. For just as Marie was unable to separate from him in life, so she is unable to separate in death. The rite of passage of leaving home is a most important rite, but not one achieved simply by moving out. It is above all a rite of inner understanding. In the following story, we come across a boy who appears to have discovered it early.

*

Every year the parents of Jesus went to Jerusalem for the Passover Festival. When Jesus was twelve years old, they went to the festival as usual. When the festival was over they started back home, but the boy Jesus stayed in Jerusalem. His parents did not know this; they thought that he was with the group, so they travelled a whole day before starting to search for him among their relatives and friends. They did not find him, so they went back to Jerusalem to look for him. On the third day they found him in the Temple, sitting with the Jewish teachers, listening to them and asking questions. All who heard him were amazed at his intelligent answers. His parents were astonished when they saw him, and his mother said to him, 'My son, why have you done this to us? Your father and I have been terribly worried trying to find you.' He answered them, 'Why did you have to look for me? Didn't you know that I had to be in my father's house?' But they did not understand his answer.

So Jesus went back with them to Nazareth, where he was obedient to them. His mother treasured all these things in her heart. Jesus grew both in body and in wisdom, gaining favour with God and [people].
Luke 2.41-52

It is the lack of apology I find most striking, and the almost chill absence of concern for his parents' feelings. Did Jesus really imagine they would be pleased with the way events had unfolded? He seems not to have been bothered either way. Whether his parents had been slack in their care of him, we do not know. It is possible this is an example of neglectful parenting. To travel a whole day without any knowledge of his whereabouts seems a little excessive. But perhaps there was a system of childcare in the wider community which could account for everything.

We do not know and since blame is generally the refuge of the frightened and hypocritical, we will not rush to join them on this occasion. In one sense it is not significant anyway, for whether they were or were not guilty of negligence that is not a concern here for Jesus. What is a concern for Jesus as his parents confront him in the Temple, is their imagined control over him.

＊

It is a good scene. Having spent three days looking for their boy, his parents at last find him in the Temple. They stand astonished and relieved in equal measure, at the events being played out before their eyes.

They can hardly be anything but moved at finding their son safe. But Jesus doesn't play their game. He doesn't for instance look sheepish and mutter something about knowing he shouldn't have done it really, and he won't do it again, promise. Neither does he run towards them to give each a huge hug, saying how much he has missed them and that they are the best mum and dad in the world. Instead, he treats them with something approaching disdain. They have spent three days fearing the worst, and yet Jesus gives them nothing to help them feel good.

As the writer winds up the incident, we can suddenly feel him beginning to worry a little, as the rudeness of the boy sinks in. And so he tells us how the boy then went back home, and was obedient to his parents. Maybe this was so, but such words sit slightly at odds with the encounter we have just witnessed. Jesus simply does not allow his parents, his own flesh and blood, either the relief at being united with him or the natural parental concern for his well-being. Rather, they are reprimanded for looking around for him, when it was perfectly obvious where he would be.

For Luke, it is a story about Jesus' blossoming messianic insight. Here was a boy of twelve impressing everyone in the Temple, the heart of Judaism, with his astounding grasp of truth. But as I watch the scene, although I am suitably amazed by the learning, I am a good deal more amazed by the fact that here is a twelve-year-old who has effectively left home already. When Jesus speaks in this scene, he speaks as one separate from the concerns of his parents; as one confident in his own identity. Their worry was their problem, not his, and the only offence committed was not his disappearance, but their attempt to control him. Jesus had done by the age of twelve what most people do not manage in a lifetime - found the freedom of separation from family.

*

It is generally reckoned that we leave home when we physically move out of the building; leaving the family residence seems to be the decisive moment in most people's eyes. According to this model, most adults have left home, and on one level this is clearly true. After all, most people are out there now having to cope on their own in some degree; do their own washing, buy their own food, clean their own toilet and stay in to meet the building contractor who is coming to have a look at the dodgy tiling. When they were growing up, their parents had to do that sort of thing. Yet most of these people have not left home. They've simply moved house.

Let us meet Amelia, who thought she had left home. She moved out of the family home at the age of seventeen and not before time as far as she was concerned. Her perception of herself was that she was an adult now, making her own way in the world, and in many ways she was, for she was soon running a company, and turning it into a success story. She found she was good at what she did, even if it was stressful. But her world unaccountably fell in when her nan died. Her nan had always been a very good place for Amelia. She had always been fond of her. But was such grief at her death really appropriate? Slowly, and fearfully, she began to realize that her parents, in contrast to her nan, had not been a good place for her. With the death of her nan, her one true place of sanctuary, she was having to confront the unthinkable.

But how could this be so? The confusion in Amelia was total. For parents were parents. Surely they must have been a good place? How could parents not be a good place? In her culture, even to pose the question was disrespectful. It was not until Amelia was 34 that she realized that her physically abusive father still held her in a vice-like emotional grip, even in his absence. And it was not until she was 39 that she realized quite how damaging her mother's silence had been throughout her childhood ordeal. Her mother could have stopped it, but chose instead to ignore it, for the sake of peace and quiet. And anyway, it suited her to have her husband around, even if it did not suit Amelia. And so everything was brushed under the carpet, to keep the family peace, whatever the cost to Amelia.

Amelia was now seeing her parents for the first time, and in her seeing, and more importantly, in her feelings of anger and rage, she was able finally to leave home, as opposed merely to changing address and getting a job. It had taken a while, but she was slowly achieving separation; better late than never.

Having now achieved some sort of separation, she is hesitantly learning to relate to her parents again, but learning to relate to them as humans, as opposed to parents. It is a different relationship, and though threatening initially to her parents, a finer one by far.

✳

In the end, it is not enough simply to be family, for family is a descriptive word, not a qualitative word. It was not enough for Amelia's family to say: 'But we are family! Don't rock the boat.' Frequently, people reserve their worst behaviour for those with whom they live. They reckon they can get away with it at home, in a way they would not in the world outside. If you can't kick the dog, there's always the child to be shown who's boss. If you are frustrated with your life, and your baby is not helping, then you deal with the child firmly. Let it learn early what frustration feels like!

Most crimes against humanity are very average, very mundane and barely warrant a thought. But such behaviour is not made any more acceptable by the fact that the victims are family and therefore don't count in the same way. Or that they will grow to understand in later life. No, it is not acceptable for me to imagine that because they are family, I do not have to try so hard. Or that I need to be tired and negative somewhere, and it can't be in the pub or at bingo or on the golf course or at work or round at my friends or in church so it has to be at home.

We've all heard or sensed the justification which goes on: 'And what are they going to do about it anyway?' they say. 'Tell me that! Go and live in a hostel? I don't think so! They like their comforts too much. And it's not as if I don't provide for them. They never go without food on the table.'

But if there is no quality of relationship, then there is nothing, family or no family. We owe no loyalty to family as such. We owe loyalty to truth, freedom, beauty, mystery, openness, and justice; we owe loyalty to kindness and gentleness, emotional and physical acceptance; we owe loyalty to innocent victims wherever they are. But we don't owe loyalty to family. Family is an arrangement we are born into, with no choice in the matter. When we are young, we must live what is, for good or ill. But one day, choice of a sort does come our way, and then, whether we stay with the family arrangement in some form or other depends purely on the quality of relating which we have experienced.

But how hard it is to separate! How hard it is to leave home, for we are conditioned to do otherwise. This was a conditioning which Jesus both knew and used to outrageous effect. Many years after the Temple incident recounted above, Jesus as an adult is trying to explain to the spiritually blind gathered around him, the radical demands of the kingdom of God. How could this best be revealed to these people, how best expressed? They are eager in their way, but seem to imagine discipleship to be something rather tame; something that can be stuck on to their existing life and assumptions.

What can be done to jerk them into consciousness? Jesus decides to shock. He names the two things that people most cling to - and declares them both to be worthless: 'No one can be a follower of mine unless they hate their father, mother, wife, children, brother and sister! And no one can be a follower of mine unless they hate their own life!' That is a big rug to pull from beneath people's feet.

There are none left standing. We are reeling as our family values are turned on their head and our passion for our own survival laughed at. Jesus invites us to count as nothing all those things society has conditioned us to count as everything; Jesus asks us to stop clinging to all those things which conditioning tells us we should cling to. We cling to family, and we cling to life. Forget them both, says Jesus, for what you cling to will kill you. Separate from these attachments and live.

*

I am reminded here of Socrates. It was he who swam against the strong tide of meaningless clinging when he remarked that 'there are so many things I have no need of'. He could say such a thing quite truthfully because of his personal sense of self. The story is told of the man who warned Socrates that people were slandering him in his absence. Socrates replied, 'Is that anything to care about? It makes so little difference to me what people do with me in my absence that they are even quite welcome to beat me up in my absence.'

He was knowingly separate, and therefore unconcerned by other people's reactions to him. Other people had power over Socrates only to the extent to which they could threaten his sense of self, and apparently, they did not threaten it at all. This did not lead to isolationism, however, or arrogant withdrawal from the flux of life. Rather, he related gladly. Socrates related well, because he didn't depend on the relation-ships and what you don't depend on, you can relate to truthfully.

*

But the words of both Socrates and Jesus have impinged little on people's lives, for they are words spoken from a higher level, and such words generally have little impact on those listening on a lower level. Words spoken from the mountain top become wilfully distorted by the valley people below, who prefer their version of the truth. So on the subject of family, no one has listened to Jesus. These mountain-top words have been 'put into perspective' by the valley people, and there-fore ignored by them, from generation unto generation.

It is a brave soul who questions the importance of family these days. 'People being negative about family is the last thing we need. We need positive input, not moaning!' Family is forbidden territory, as a true story from Germany illustrates with some savagery:

In 1987, a man called Niklas Frank wrote an article in the magazine *Stern* condemning his father. His father had been Hans Frank, the Nazi Governor-General of Poland, from 1939 to 1945. In that post, he had carried out deliberate torture and murder on a massive scale. Among other things, he had general oversight of at least three death camps whose only reason for existence was the killing of unwanted racial and ethnic types. His son's article forty years later pulled no punches. It did not attempt to be even-handed in any way. It did not attempt to understand the actions of his father, nor did it make any attempt to forgive him. He just condemned the life of this man.

Such condemnation of a father by a son is rare. But that is not why I tell this story. I tell this story because of what followed the article being published; and in particular, the reaction it provoked in the letter pages. The feeling among many was that whatever the father had done, it was not for the son to say such things. As one reader said, 'No matter what the father has done, his foulest deed was un-doubtedly the procreation of this perverse monster of a son.' Another reader came to similar conclusions: 'Anyone else is free to, should, in fact, write this article, but not the son. In doing so, he acts just as inhumanly as his father once did.' These are remarkable statements and almost demand a pause to reflect on their implications. I have to stop writing; and you may want to stop reading, to feel the disturbing forces at work here.

One thing is clear though: to condemn evil is apparently as bad as the evil itself, if it happens to be evil perpetrated by a member of the family. What is unsettling is the power of social and probably religious programming at work among these people. Family is declared by them to be a different zone, where different rules apply; where loyalty is placed above truth, and the honour of the family above respect for others.

The message here is that families should keep quiet, should not question things, but idealize the ghastly. And if Herr Frank was not allowed to question the past, given the nature of his father's atrocities, what hope for us whose family have perhaps been involved in less infamous activity? And so we keep quiet, even though we have been greatly affected by things done to us, and attitudes imposed upon us. We stay quiet for it is unkind, unfair and disloyal even to raise the matter. After all, family is family, as the readers of *Stern* made very clear. And we don't want to be deemed perverse monsters by others.

We are some way here from the attitudes of the boy Jesus in the Temple.

*

As we reflect on separation from family, we cannot help but reflect on self-image and self-identity, which enable healthy separation to take place.

Self-image has very little to do with our social position in life. We might clean toilets and travel on the bus, or we might be prime minister and travel in expensive limousines, but these are irrelevancies, for our self-image arises from our memory strands. These take us back to our earliest days, to our interactions with those who had primary care of us and in particular, the mother figure.

These strands of memory have a life beyond our consciousness, but remember profoundly, discerning well and knowingly the quality of relationships which were ours in those earliest of times. The self-image we emerge with as adults contains all these memories, whether from our bike or our private jet.

But though such knowledge may exist in our body, it does not exist in our consciousness, which means that as we grow, we are quite unaware of it. Gradually, however, they crystallize into core attitudes which we carry with us into every situation and unknowingly live from. While these attitudes remain beyond our consciousness, we can neither examine them nor feel them, and there is no escape from their power. As slaves to the past, we find ourselves unable to live easily in the present; struggling to touch the diamond of free engagement with the now.

And so it was that an amazing thing happened: the head teacher of a school resigned when she was doing a brilliant job. How did it happen? Week in, week out, she had worked wonders in this difficult setting. She had always wanted to make a difference to something or someone in her life, and now she was doing so. Unfortunately, however, she could never celebrate what she did. Others told her she was doing well, but she couldn't feel this herself, and worried constantly that she had done the wrong thing or that she was worth nothing and that no one liked her.

Sometimes she broke out in posturing anger and sometimes in inappropriate self-aggrandisement, but mostly it was just crippling worry. She was living and working from her memory strands, which discerned nothing helpful or nurturing in the mirroring of herself by her parents. She grew up superficially bright and vivacious, but it was a brittle show and hollow within, and life finds out the brittle and hollow. The official reason she resigned was the stress of the job, but that was an irrelevance. She was a brilliantly gifted head who resigned because she had never left home.

*

There are those who regret the fact that they did not say the things they would like to have said to a family member during their living years. They were never quite able to connect, to seize the moment, and now the time is past and the moment gone becomes an unspoken eternity. Some of these people will have held back out of politeness towards their elders, towards their parents. Maybe they also feared rocking the ordered and fragile family boat. Or perhaps it was a different issue - perhaps they wanted to say something good and kind, something appreciative and warm, but were simply too embarrassed to do so, because the family didn't do emotional things like that. Good boys and girls stay in line, and for them, it was important to be a good boy or a good girl.

Others again held back not in politeness or fear but in rage. Reduced to wordless frustration in the face of their family, they are trapped in the prison of rebellion and unresolved feelings.

None of these people have achieved separation, from which true relating grows; for all are still struggling with their identity. The first group have opted to merge their identity with that of the family, while the second group have been forced to define their self-image by anger. One set lives fearful of war, while the other set lives by conducting war, and neither know peace within; for neither have yet acquired their own identity.

When we are able to recover our identity from the battlefields of our earliest interactions, it is then that we can enjoy the freedom of the independent. Independence is not indifference - but the place from which we can freely choose to relate. When we can know ourselves apart from our mother and father, brothers and sisters, uncles and aunts, grandparents and cousins; when we can smell the coffee of life in our own way, and not as we have been taught to smell it, then we are coming home.

*

We are told most parents just want their children to be happy. They don't want fame or fortune for them - just that they are happy in whatever they choose to do. It is a fine sentiment. Yet if you scratch the surface a little, it becomes apparent that many of these parents want their children to be happy – but only on their terms. 'Be happy, but remember you are family and all that entails. We have high hopes for you, and we know you will not let us down.'

If this desire for happiness in their children were genuine, then the first thing the parents would do would be to make some very specific apologies about the childhood they created for them. This is a unique conversation with each child, for no children are treated the same. The conversation to be had with my sister will not be the same as the conversation to be had with me.

People sometimes imagine that parenting is equal in a home; that it is the same for one brother as another, but this is not the case. Each child is born into a different family setting, a different chemistry of relationships and different attitudes from the carers, for life is a moving river.

Perhaps the first child was born into her mother's depression, which was not the case for the second. Or perhaps in another family, unlike the first three, the mother didn't want the fourth child, but had been coerced by the father. In such circumstances, she resents the presence of this new arrival, and so this fourth child might have to do more to win her approval than the others; he will certainly feel the cold winds of frustration in the mother, should he be difficult. Families are not places of equality.

Take Vincent Van Gogh, for instance, and Vincent Van Gogh. It isn't a misprint. Vincent Van Gogh died tragically when young, and so in order to remember him, his religious parents decided to name their next boy after him, so when born, he too was called Vincent Van Gogh. This was the man who went on to paint pictures which were ridiculed and ignored during his life - he sold only two - but have achieved some fame since.

His childhood was deeply unhappy, for apart from the stern religiosity of his parents, they never forgave him for not being his dead elder brother. His dead elder brother - unreachable in the grave that Vincent was made to visit regularly - was the boy and man the younger Vincent never could be. Vincent even shared a birthday with his elder brother. The young Vincent was not an individual with an identity of his own, but a poor replica of someone else, someone better, someone untouchable in their perfection, someone who in death could never mess things up.

When in later life he moved to Arles in the South of France, Van Gogh discovered there a 'kingdom of light' and stunning colour. He was born again as an artist, with the ordinary becoming extraordinary to him in this new setting. He painted everything - cafes, children, streets, night, people, countryside, sunflowers, even his bedroom.

The cold northern skies of childhood were no more, and a huge vitality overtook him, sending him into remarkable creativity.

But the child is the parent of the adult, and the scars of inadequacy remained. He could throw off the religious shackles of his parents, but he could not throw off the cloak of despair which clung to his inner parts. If your parents did not celebrate your life as something wonderful and good, then it is hard in later years for you to do so. It is significant that Van Gogh never signed his paintings with that name. When he emerged as an artist, he was simply 'Vincent'. Not a single painting or drawing from his adult years bears the family name. He rationalized it by claiming that foreigners could not pronounce 'Van Gogh', which may well have been true. But it was not the profoundest truth concerning this matter. By this simple act, Vincent was cutting himself off from both his father and the entire Van Gogh family culture and belief.

Instead, he was going to find his own way in life. 'I am not a Van Gogh!' he declared, after calling his father obstinate, unintelligent, icy cold and narrow-minded.

He tried to redeem the situation in his life, constantly falling and failing in love, trying to form a new family, a family of affinity. He attempted also to create a community of artists, an idea close to his heart. Paul Gauguin joined him in the 'Yellow House' and there was companionship of a sort until a furious row destroyed the fragile relationship and Gauguin left.

Van Gogh poured his feelings into his art. Perhaps there has never been a painter who painted more profoundly from his state of mind. As has been said, 'He carried the sun in his head and a hurricane in his heart... he did not paint with his hands but with his naked senses... painting himself within those fiery clouds... in those twisting trees that seem to yell to heaven, in the frightening vastness of his plains.' As he himself stated in his final letter to his brother Theo, he risked everything for his work, even madness and eventually his life.

It was a sort of madness, but there was no choice, for he had to pursue that which gave life to the moment, that which helped him touch the vibrancy of the now, which gave him a sense of self different from that imposed on him in his early years. For Van Gogh, this desperate bid for freedom was played out through the painting of feeling, both the torment and the hope. The hope he expressed in the colour yellow.

At Van Gogh's funeral, some of his most recent canvases were hung around the room where his body lay, while on the coffin hung a single white drape and hundreds of flowers: sunflowers, which were his favourite, yellow dahlias and other yellow flowers. Yellow for him was the colour of the light he hoped to find in himself and in others. The individual who probably offered him most hope was his brother Theo - a blood relative and friend who was endlessly generous to Vincent financially and in the encouragement he gave. He could not cure Vincent of his troubles, and often received little by way of thanks from him. But he was a friend amid them in simple and practical ways. Vincent placed his own torment on the canvas, ever the stranger on earth, the stunted plant fighting for life.

Yet for someone who saw art as a record of 'the universality of suffering' and who is often seen as a tragic figure, he also painted much beauty along the way, and we need not be surprised. Those who visit the darkness have within them the capacity for discoveries of amazing light, painter or no painter. In this book, we do not avoid the bleak, or ease its impact with soft-coloured words. But we continue on, feeling all things, for we keep glimpsing the beauty which honesty creates. Van Gogh painted his despair, but created light. To his parents, he was never as good as the brother who didn't live; to his brother Theo, he was family, who needed help; and to the rest of the world, in time, he was a swirling and courageous gift from God.

*

Parents help their children best when they face the past, and reflect on what they were unable to offer the dependent baby in those early times; and therefore help the child to see the roots of so much of the quiet unhappiness in their life now. There is nothing which cannot ultimately be mended, and there is nothing to fear except denial. The white dove of possibility hovers always.

Sadly, however, the parent's desire for their children's happiness does not usually include such brave actions. When most parents say they want their children to be happy, they are merely saying they them-selves want to be happy. Children are perceived as extensions of the parents; as those who must fall in line with that perception and serve that overriding requirement. After all, their own parents never apolo-gized to them, and it hasn't done them any harm! The very idea is lu-dicrous. Toughen up a bit!

But you cannot wish someone's happiness and not apologize; and you cannot wish someone's happiness, yet refuse to let them go.

It would be healthier, and less open to manipulation, if parents wished not so much that their children might be happy, but that their children might be free: and in particular, free from them. What a beautiful wish that would be. And strangely enough, if one was able to wish that for them, they might actually be not only free, but also happy as well.

How refreshing to find parents who wish their children freedom to separate from all things, including themselves, in order that they might in time relate to all things. For you can only relate to that from which you are separate.

Rilke was in this territory when he said that the prime calling in mar-riage was for each of the partners to protect the solitude of the other. If you don't know who you are separately, then how can you possibly live together in anything other than pain and frustration? As the mystics say, 'Knowingly separate, gladly relating.'

*

This is not a book about parenting, but about reclaiming the won-derful child which poor parenting destroyed - for beautiful families grow not out of parenting manuals but from reclaimed childhoods. It is for this reason that I write as a son, and not as a parent, for it is with the child's eyes we need to reflect on these things. Whatever our age, we come to this subject first and foremost as children.

Much may have happened to us in life since those days, and we may have acquired many other titles and areas of expertise along the way. But the child remains our primary identity, for it was as children that our defining formation took place. So we may also be a parent or a grandparent, a bank manager or director of social services or perhaps a nursery nurse, a professor of theology or an enormously successful mushroom farmer soon to expand into organic parsnips. But these are secondary identities, and ones we are liable to struggle with, unless we have come to terms with the daughter or the son who we are.

I once met myself as a child in my imagination. It had been suggested that I try it, but I was wary. I could not remember being more fearful of a meeting than the one proposed. In the end, I did it. I sat quietly with a photo of myself on a beach, and then in my imagination, I went along to meet this character. I imagined meeting my little self on the beach, like in the holiday photo from way back.

Initially, there was awkwardness, so the adult I suggested to the child I that we went out in a boat together. Once in the boat, the adult I had to make most of the conversation, for the child I was suspicious. The adult even found himself disliking the child, impatient for the little person to be something different. The adult judged the child's stupid clothes, fat little body and awkward manner. The child was probably familiar with that reaction. But given time, the adult's judgemental irritation began to fade, and was replaced by warm feelings towards this small person, and a sense of camaraderie and connection. On meeting, the distance between the two had been huge. It was as if we didn't know each other. But in the end, the adult I was crying at the sense of reconciliation, for this child was the father of the adult.

We returned to the beach and said goodbye. Perhaps we will meet again one day. Perhaps one day we will dance. I don't know how we allowed ourselves to be separated in the first place.

Separation from family

PART TWO

Feelings are going to matter in our journey towards freedom. We may not welcome feelings, for they can be debilitating. But if we are careful towards ourselves, they are more friend than foe. Indeed, there is no path to freedom which does not involve authentic feeling.

Every feeling tells a story, but they are not always stories we want to hear. Our feelings not only reveal much about the person we have become – they also give clues as to why we have become as we are. This is why we are encouraged, at the end of each day, to listen gently back to our feelings. What, for instance, made me happy today, shooting sunshine through my soul? What made me sad? What hit me like a cold dark cloud? What frightened me? Why did I find that particular conversation so unnerving? What made me feel uncomfortable or trapped or impatient? Why that sudden sense of peace?

To consider our feelings in this way is not to worship them. Rather, it is an attempt to understand ourselves, for each feeling is part of the paper trail back to our forgotten but formative years.

One of the reasons we pay little attention to our feelings is that we imagine our particular feelings to be inevitable. 'Of course I felt angry when they said that - how could I feel otherwise?'

Or, 'Of course I'm envious of him - who wouldn't be?'

Or, 'Of course I'm peaceful now my cat has returned.'

Or, 'Of course the sun makes me happy!'

But there is no 'of course' in these matters, for there is nothing inevitable about our feelings. That which made me see red today may well not have upset you in the slightest; and that which sent me spiralling into euphoria may have left you completely cold. But then you are constantly upset and intimidated by a person who has no power to hurt me at all. I can't understand your over- reaction to them. Your issues are other than mine, for we grew in different soil. Our panic buttons and alarm bells are found in different rooms; our places of pleasure down different corridors.

Feelings are a paper trail of clues about our unique past. My feelings help me to piece together my history, which I appreciate, because no one else is telling it to me.

*

Feelings are not the preserve of some but the truth of all. Yet few handle them well. At one extreme are those who live life on the roller-coaster of feeling, almost glorying in emotional reactions. Their inner life is a soap opera of ups and downs. Moods have an enormous power over these people and they live each mood to the full, whether it be celebration, grief, wistfulness, anger, hilarity, resentment or depression. They are their mood, invariably feeling something intensely. 'That is the sort of person I am,' they will say, 'heart on my sleeve!'

But that is not the person they are. That is the person they have become, and there is a difference, for when they were born they were not like that. Their true self has no relationship to their moods. Those most obviously controlled by their feelings often behave in a manner which suggests they have no idea where these feelings come from, like riders on wild horses thrown this way and that, by forces they do not know. To this degree, it is often phoney feeling, hysterical escapism.

Within such people is a deep snake pit of unexamined emotions. Out of this writhing mass of repressed material, the snakes are forever leaping upwards, and seizing on current events. But they are attacking the wrong objects and displaying themselves in inappropriate places.

Meet Billy. I know Billy as a polite and easy-going young man. But then I listen to him on the doorstep of his friend's house. Billy and his mate had been part of a trio of friends, but now the trio has been shattered by the other two falling out and Billy can't cope. He has never been able to handle conflict and this is conflict very close to home. It terrifies him. Suddenly a snake is leaping upwards inside him, and he explodes in a tantrum on the doorstep of his friend, who he blames for the split.

Billy is eighteen years old and usually appears the calmest of folk, but behaves here as though he is still in the terrible-twos in almost primal desperation. He shouts and rants and is physically threatening. Like a flash flood, the tantrum is over as quickly as it appeared. The snake returns to the pit. But the damage is done. His long-buried terror of conflict, placed in him in his early years by his carers, has spilled out inappropriately in the face of a friend, doing terrible things to the friendship.

Billy wants to mend it straightaway of course. He was shouting a minute ago, but now he is desperate to make up. His friend, however, can't quite see it that way.

The feelings of anger and helplessness inside Billy are extremely important. He has always been afraid of owning up to his strength, for fear of upsetting his parents and bringing their disapproval on himself. So he has repressed it, and seen it only occasionally in its distorted form - as anger.

Yet even as he loses control, he is touching the path back to his true self. To shout and to rage is the healthy reaction of any child, against the psychological, emotional or physical assaults of the adult. It is just this rage, declared forbidden at home, which has exploded uncontrollably in the wrong place, on the doorstep of another person's home; it is this rage which has been directed against the wrong object, his best friend.

Large outpourings of emotion, whether public or private, are rarely honest affairs. They are unexamined feelings attaching themselves to the wrong objects. Every feeling tells a story, but people do not wish to follow the path that leads back to the true nature of their grief, and so live lives of ultimately dishonest and foolish reaction.

At the opposite end of the emotional spectrum, are those who struggle with the idea of feeling.

They squirm in horror in the midst of emotion, and are quick to condemn the theatricals of the hysteric.

But those who are repulsed by such outbursts may also be some way from home themselves. For they are generally those who raised the drawbridge on feeling a long time ago, and retired inside their sparse castle of supposed rationality, where they feel secure, if a little cut off.

The unanswered question in their lives is this: why did they raise the drawbridge in the first place? What happened in their early days that frightened them so badly that they could survive only by shutting all feeling out? This is not a natural thing for a child to do, for feelings of love, warmth and acceptance are the most wonderful things. How good it is when another human receives you completely. Who would raise the drawbridge on a feeling like that? But if such things were not available, you might very well raise the drawbridge. There must have been a particular reason why these people as children decided that they could not face their feelings. And so they did the only thing they could to alleviate the pain.

Imagine the feelings of little Vincent van Gogh, living in that particular climate of cold rejection. His parents, and particularly his mother, were his only world on whom he depended in all things and in whom he hoped beyond hope. His feelings towards them were open and endless, aching to trust, and longing to find life-creating love in their gaze. But no feelings of warmth were returned, no mirrored longing expressed.

When you are helplessly small and all you ever wanted is not given to you, there is nothing to do but to close down, for how else can one so young survive? These feelings cannot be faced, so they must be banished. Up goes the drawbridge. Feelings? Emotional nonsense!

Such a life will always be looking for authentic love, but at the same time be terrified of finding it. For what should they then do? Can they risk disappointment again? Aren't they better off just looking after themselves, something they have had to learn from a young age and have come to trust in as a way of life? They will be desperate to be enveloped in physical, spiritual and emotional acceptance. They will long for the hands of time to be wound back that they might receive now what they never received when young. But at the same time, they will struggle, in fear, to respond if they are fortunate enough to find it being offered.

Until they dare open the box of what has been, such people will remain in their dreary castle of rationality, where nothing of value can be known; and in their continued blocking of the past, they become stupid in the present. They may boast a narrow intellectual intelligence, but they have no more emotional intelligence than the hysterical souls they condemn, and it is emotional intelligence which is required in order to relate, whether to God or human.

*

There can be no value-judgement placed on our feelings. It is unhelpful to be pleased about some and feel bad about others. No feeling is virtuous and no feeling is a crime. To feel a negative feeling - be it anger, doubt, jealousy, fear, hate or despair - is not wrong.

The feeling inside you is merely a symptom, a messenger on behalf of a deeper truth buried within us. The feeling itself is not evil but a departure point for exploration.

Take the feeling of jealousy, for instance. It is an unpleasant and crippling condition, a life-destroyer, but not wrong in itself. It is merely a sign that we are unhappy people; a revelation exposing discontent in a significant area of our lives. Why else would we feel so destructively towards that person, who has what we want? Jealousy is a most absurd idea to those who are happy, for they have all that they want. They are content. So when jealousy appears, it is a surface truth, pointing to the more fundamental truth of unhappiness. To this extent it is a friend, bidding us investigate the cancer within, and pursue the grail of a more joyful life. There is no feeling we need fear acknowledging.

So when feelings knock on our door, whatever they may be, the wise will answer the door and face the guest, wanted or unwanted. God can work with such people as these are people who face the truth. But God cannot work with those who do not answer the door, and remain closed to the truth of their feelings. This is the territory of denial, which is perhaps the worst crime in the world, for it is the crime which makes all other crimes possible.

Denial of feelings past and present; the refusal to trace them to their roots and the blind and misplaced punishment of those around us which results - this is Satan's territory. And it is such people who do damage in the world.

*

How can feelings help us to discover our past? If I say that my shirt is green, it is a clue to its colour, though far from specific. There are, after all, many shades of green. But you know more than you did before. You know, at least, that my shirt is not red, orange or indigo and there is some comparison here with our feelings. They may not give us all the details we want, but they do give us a general picture. If, for instance, we feel awkward when held, or push away even as we reach out, it suggests that no one held us very joyfully when we were small. We may not be able to remember specifics, but it is an odd thing to find difficult, when to be held in safe and loving arms is so beautiful. This is a feeling whose outcomes can destroy adult relationships, but its origins are way back.

Or listen to the woman who at the age of seventeen met a man at a bus stop, talked for ten minutes, then went back to his place for sex. Neither wanted more than that; neither wanted to exchange phone numbers afterwards. They never met again. Thinking back on that evening, and listening to her feelings at the time, she can remember feeling reassured by the experience; the intense if brief sense of value which arises from enjoyable sex. That is where the paper trail starts. But it leads back to her inner scream for reassurance, a reassurance which, for some reason, she didn't possess within, and which caused her without a moment's hesitation to risk going back to a stranger's home. What happened at the bus stop and after was primarily about her past.

Or consider the woman who tried hard to please her father, but realized one day that she could not imagine crying at his funeral; in fact, whisper it quietly, but she would probably be relieved. This apparently unnatural and embarrassing feeling was not created out of nothing; there must have been a reason. A child does not naturally feel such things about a parent. Every child is born into the world with a strong desire for trusting adventure, and an energy for the giving and receiving of love. When the adventure breaks down and the energy dies, there is always a reason. The good news is that the woman has been brave enough to notice it, and now more clues are appearing.

No feeling is either a virtue or a crime. Rather, each feeling is a clue to something done; every feeling, the beginning of a path to something which once happened when we were tiny and very absorbent of experience.

*

It is not the present which causes us to feel as we do. It is our past. Every feeling we have now has deep roots in our past, for that is where we learnt how to feel. This also means that every feeling we now experience is probably closely related to our family in some way or other.

What we tend to do is to project these feelings, most of which we are unaware of, on to the world around us. And so it is that some people will like you for no obvious reason, and some people will dislike you for no obvious reason, and this is why some relationships are almost effortlessly easy while others are always difficult and painful. People project on to others the good and bad from their past. If you happen to be the recipient of the good, then be grateful, but don't take it personally; if you are a recipient of the bad, then be patient, but don't take it personally. This is territory over which we have very little control.

Charlie was always in trouble at school. She had a problem with authority. But it wasn't all authority she struggled with, only particular authority: authority she had no respect for. She could not stomach even the smallest order from such a person, and wouldn't obey, whatever the personal cost to herself. She had little control over the feelings of anger inside her, or the rage that even small requests engendered in her. There was a beautiful strength in Charlie, but distorted with pain, it turned to rage. She made more than one teacher cry. To the outsider, she is just another out-of-control teenager, who needs to learn some discipline.

Were these particularly poor teachers? No. They were simply teachers whose personality and practice reminded her of her inconsistent mother, whose irrational and selfish discipline she had had to endure as a child with no opportunity for redress. The teachers who reminded her of her gentler if slightly ineffectual father had an easier time of it. She couldn't warm to any authority. But she would not take on this second sort in open hostility. Daddy was OK.

It is hard for the teachers not to take it personally, but they were latecomers on the scene in Charlie's psyche. It was impossible for her to cooperate with them, once the lethal connection had been made between them and her past. Not that Charlie understood any of this at the time.

✻

Feelings, when they appear in us, are best noticed and pondered on. Everyday feelings, such as frustration, happiness, loneliness, irritation, anger, sadness, freedom, worry, unease, fear, depression, stress, despair or peace - these are there to be noticed, greeted and pondered: what made them appear, however fleetingly? We are not judging our feelings in any way. Neither are we taking them too seriously, for they are the most ephemeral of things, with no life other than that of a parasite. We are just interested observers, looking to see where they came from. I am suddenly happy or suddenly sad. But why do I feel that now? What needs in me do these feelings expose? Each feeling we greet as a friend and a truth teller.

✻

In the end, we will need to go further. It is good to notice and observe but we will need to go further and permit the feelings buried within us to come to the surface in all their awful but liberating power. We will need to put aside our reflections - however astute they may be - and go to the place of pain; the place where our child within dares to speak what it has never dared speak before.

Amid a recent disaster which caught the imagination of the world, I was struck by the various responses from church leaders. Some pondered reflectively, from their desks or behind studio microphones, on the theological implications of this terrible event; others busied themselves with rallying the troops, organizing aid, comic book heroes

38

making a difference to a sad world. But the only authentic voice I heard was that of the bishop in the midst of the disaster, who just said: 'We are desperate. We are crying, and we are hungry.' His words were almost child-like in their simplicity, and the mark of someone close to the epicentre of the trauma.

It is one thing to observe; quite another thing to feel. It is one thing to reflect from distance on a wall of fire, and quite another to walk through it. When we begin to allow our child to tell their story, we too will stand in the epicentre of the trauma; we too will have to walk through the wall of fire - the fire of feeling. Ultimately, it is feeling and not wisdom which lead us to the clearing.

There is no going round this fire; only the going through it. It is the place where we allow ourselves to feel those things we have never before allowed ourselves to feel. Others may surround us with support, and it may be that a particular soul helps us with our journey. But in the end, they can only encourage from the sidelines. The walk through the fire is inevitably a lonely one, for it is our true self that we are reclaiming, our originally hopeful and open life that we are seeking out. No one can seek it for us. There are some things we have to do for ourselves. And the hardest of these is to feel truly.

This adventure is for everyone. Sometimes if extreme examples of unfortunate behaviour are given, or famous people are used as examples, we can imagine that as our lives are nothing like that, we need do nothing other than consign such things to our 'interesting psychological histories' pile, and move on. But this is to miss the point. Whether or not we perceive ourselves to be the victims of abuse is quite irrelevant; what is relevant is that we free ourselves of the conditioning of our past, and in particular, the conditioning of our family set-up.

We need to leave home not only physically, but emotionally and spiritually, in order to discover the vibrancy of the glory within us – a glory often hidden but never lost; the glory which is particular to ourselves, yet eagerly waiting to relate to others.

First we will seek to feel the pushed-away things. And in a while, the change: instead of our feelings taking responsibility for our lives, our lives will take responsibility for our feelings.

*

How do you respond to this? You might say, 'I take your point, but really, I have nothing to complain about!' The process of separation, however, is not about you having something to complain about. (Though you might pause to wonder why you are quite so insistent that you don't. Who or what do you fear?) Rather, the process of separation is concerned with understanding the forces at work in our formation that we might move more freely, consciously and merrily in the world. Why should others suffer through our ignorance of our personal history, the cause of so much of our quiet and unknowing mistreatment of others? And why should we ourselves suffer from the confused entanglements in our past? Entanglements can make forgiveness hard, loving hollow and guilt remorseless - and all because our boundaries are so blurred.

As the night watch waits for the dawn, so will we watch for the clues in our feelings. And in time, when the season is right, we will feel things that perhaps we would prefer not to, in order that we might separate ourselves from the rotting and unexamined alliances of convenience which we have settled into. And then perhaps we will begin truly to relate again.

Maybe in the early days there will be a chill feeling to our separation, just as there was in the words of the boy Jesus in the Temple. He was very young here, and still growing into his virtues; a virtue he could see only through a glass darkly at this point in his life. Growing into something precious is not a smooth ride of easy adaptation, but an awkward and jerking progression, as new inner vistas bring new external challenges. But clearly even at this young age, the boy Jesus could feel where freedom and authenticity lay and where therefore he must be. As we know, life is difficult, but not complicated.

First there is the discernment of where life lies, and then the choosing of it. Jesus discerned his calling, chose it and acted on it. It wasn't what his parents discerned to be good or chose for him. Indeed, they were most upset by it. But then it wasn't their life. It was his.

*

Between one thing becoming another thing, there is a time of change. There is an inner dying, a sense of withdrawal from the world, in order to understand the time; a cocoon-like retreat from former pressures in order to reflect on what is necessary now. Change may ultimately show itself in many external ways, but good change will always be directed from within, and arise from solitude.

Between the caterpillar and the butterfly, is the experience of the chrysalis. Those around us may find it hard to cope with such a state in us, with our apparent disintegration, for ours is an extrovert and doing society. 'What are you doing?' they ask, and we can feel the pressure ourselves. We feel we should be performing, delivering, holding things together. But when the moment comes, the caterpillar has no choice. And neither do we. I can do nothing in the world if there is no I - and until I separate, there isn't.

We enter the chrysalis, in whatever form it takes, to pass from one state to another - to be able to say, 'I am.'

A significant stage in this process is the battle of the inner consciences. We seem to have two consciences available to us. The first is that of our social conditioning, created primarily by our family, and in particular the parental attitudes into which we were born and in which our absorbent early years were lived. Our second conscience is that of our deepest insight; the undamaged perception of reality latent in all people, and which a mature human being will find increasingly compelling. The first conscience is a borrowed conscience, second hand. The second conscience is core conscience, mined from the deepest places within.

The possession of these two different consciences makes for a struggle within us. They appear to be at war and often saying opposite things. To which conscience do I listen? To which do I bow? It is particularly hard during the process whereby authority within us is gradually passed from the first to the second. Our borrowed conscience has attached itself to every sinew within, and will not give up without a fight; while our core conscience is initially a fragile affair, glimpsed only faintly at first, in times of intense seeing. It is impossible to live comfortably from both, for the two will argue. Part of forsaking family is an increasing dependence on our core conscience, which may not always appear practical, but has the greater ring of truth and is a better light for our journey.

And as we cease to be directed by others, we become increasingly directed from within. We do not give people authority over us, but learn gradually to listen to the inner voice. As Jesus said, we must call no one father on earth, for we have only one father and he is in heaven. We may respect others, but we will allow no authority figure to decide for us, or issue orders on our behalf. It must be our own heart that speaks, drawing from an ever growing awareness of, and closeness to, our core conscience. Like long-buried treasure, it is a wonderful discovery.

✻

Separation from others can of course feel and appear uncaring, for it goes against the grain of our social conditioning. But it goes with the grain of ultimate truth and beauty. See the distinct colours of the arching rainbow across the sky: red, orange, yellow, green, blue, indigo and violet. Pour those colours into one pot, mix them around, and they will look like nothing except a brown mess. Yet separate together in the heavens, distinct but relating, they become the wonderful promise of better things ahead.

Ignorance among family

Meet Stuart. As an infant, he was caught up in the unlived dreams and nightmares of his parents, which they projected onto him. They did not consider his life to be his own, but an extension of theirs. He therefore gave up trying to live his own life. His feelings and needs had been rejected, for the adults were too busy with themselves. He had been declared unimportant. His own glory, hopeful and aspiring, had not been deemed a matter of consequence by the family authorities.

In order to cope with this devastating blow, Stuart developed a persona through which to live his life. His true self was too hurt to proceed, but behind a persona, there could be survival. It creaked a little in its early days, but as time went by, he got better at the pretence. He wouldn't allow himself to be angry, because that would be wrong in his eyes, though sometimes anger would spill out at inappropriate moments in a negative and raging sort of way. Where did that come from?! Generally though, his careful nonchalance and pretended freedom were accepted by the world.

Indeed, so well did he wear the mask that he himself came to believe it was true. Not only had his parents been ignorant and ignoring of his needs. Now he was too.

Here now is another story of someone enduring ignorance but a different course of action is taken.

After this, Jesus travelled in Galilee; he did not want to travel in Judea, because the Jewish authorities there were wanting to kill him. The time for the Festival of Shelters was near, so Jesus' brothers said to him, 'Leave this place and go to Judea, so that your followers will see the things that you are doing. No one hides what he is doing if he wants to be well known. Since you are doing these things, let the world know about you!' (Not even his brothers believed in him.) Jesus said to them, 'The right time for me has not yet come. Any time is right for you. The world cannot hate you, but it hates me, because I keep telling it that its ways are bad. You go on to the festival. I am not going to this festival, because the right time has not come for me.' He said this and then stayed on in Galilee.

After his brothers had gone to the festival, Jesus also went; however, he did not go openly, but secretly.

John 7.1-10

In this rather bleak episode in the family life of Jesus, we find him discovering how little his brothers understand the shape of his life or the nature of his aspirations.

There is sometimes the assumption that families are the place where we are understood, but this is not necessarily so. Often ignorant about themselves, it should not surprise us that families can be very ignorant about us as well.

This is how it was for Jesus, at a time of difficulty and vulnerability in his life. A man facing death-threats from people hostile to his every move can find it a very lonely world. It can become lonelier still, when you walk into a brick wall of family ignorance; when it becomes clear to you that your nearest and dearest do not really know you at all.

His brothers presume, for instance, that he wants to be well known in the world; that he desires fame and fortune like everyone else. Perhaps they do this deliberately to upset him, for at no point in his life does Jesus give any hint of such a wish. Indeed, it is a travesty of his calling and all the more hurtful a suggestion for that. But then, families know how to hurt, particularly when they are angry or threatened. The negative intelligence of adults exists primarily to seek out the weak places in others, and this often reveals itself in calculated and deliberate misunderstanding. Such intelligence is not virtuous but it is insightful. Maybe it was at play here.

*

We don't know many specifics about Jesus' family, but it seems likely that his father Joseph was older than Mary, and had died before Jesus' public ministry began. There is no mention of him, for instance, at the wedding in Cana which Mary attended. Indeed, there is no mention of him anywhere save in the stories around Jesus' birth.

With Jesus as the eldest son, it is likely that he stayed at home to support the family, working in the carpentry trade until he was thirty, until an inner calling pressed him to leave. I think we can confidently infer that none of Jesus' family thought it was time for him to leave.

Whatever may have been in the past, however, any support Jesus had given to the family in his first thirty years was not returned now. Jesus is here misunderstood by his brothers, whether deliberately or unwittingly, and desiring to be free from their exhausting company, he responds by deceiving them about his intentions. He sends them off to the festival in Judea, saying that he was staying in Galilee. This was a lie, for he did not intend to stay on in Galilee but went to the festival in his own time, in disguise and happily free of his family's advice.

*

It is significant that when describing this brief encounter, John goes out of his way to make clear that the brothers of Jesus did not believe in him. John effectively declares them, his family, to be just another branch of the opposition. As this perception cannot be directly inferred from the incident recorded here, it must have been a knowledge John had from other experiences in Jesus' life, common gossip to those in the know. This incident merely gave him the chance to put it on record. Certainly he infuses this incident with dysfunction. The painful present for Jesus among his family, according to John, was disbelief and misunderstanding.

We are fragile souls, craving affirmation. How we are lifted by praise and knocked down by criticism! Like a desert longing for rain, our insecure personality longs to be valued by others. When we do not receive value, we are inclined either to collapse or lash out, and such might have been Jesus' response here. Fortunately, however, he was secure enough in himself to know he could trust his own counsel, in the face of ill-conceived family pressure. He knew the path he would take, and felt no compulsion to tell them, for they would not understand. They may have played together when young, inventing games with wood shapes from their father's off-cuts, but that was then, their father was dead and things now were rather different. Jesus must make his own way in life from here on - and choose confidantes other than those he grew up with.

*

We are given no clues as to how Jesus felt about this incident. We know what he decided to do, but we do not know the feelings which surged through him on the way to this decision. It is hard, though, if you sense that your family never quite believes in you, and struggles to affirm you in your growing sense of self and gift. It can dampen confidence, denying to you the joyful exploration of trying to find out who you are, and denying to the world your particular genius.

It is sad to meet people who are so much smaller than they might have been, emotionally curled up in almost foetus-like regression.

Families are influential both in giving wings and in clipping them. In this instance, Jesus' wings are scratched and ripped by the bitter and destructive claws of family negativity. For someone already insecure in themselves it could have been decisive. The insecure are felled by the smallest of events, and the realization that someone you thought close to you does not understand you can leave you emotionally winded and struggling for breath.

Later in his life, in the garden of Gethsemane shortly before he died, Jesus was overcome with self-doubt. He begged for his cup of suffering to be taken from him. But it cannot have been the first time he was tempted to throw in the towel. How weary Jesus must have been for much of the time, and how very alone. But Jesus was secure enough to know that, sometimes, alone was all right.

*

Despite the moving football anthem, 'You'll never walk alone', in one sense, we do the walk of life profoundly alone. We are born alone, we die alone, and in between we live in a world which is not greatly moved either to care about us or to understand us.

This may initially sound a little bleak, but it is nothing of the kind, for there is nothing to fear in the alone if it becomes solitude - which is loneliness redeemed. Once we understand that to walk alone in some measure is inevitable, and accept that it is entirely manageable then relating to others becomes a good deal more joyful. We appreciate them, but we do not depend on them for our well-being or trust them for our happiness.

People sometimes punish themselves for not being able to trust others - but this guilt is a mistake. Trust in another is not in itself a virtue. For Jesus to trust his brothers in this situation would not have been a virtue, but a dereliction of duty and trust misplaced. It is a virtue to be trustworthy certainly - but to trust others is foolishness, for no one can be trusted.

Why is this? Why can't people be trusted? There is not one single reason, but three obviously come to mind.

First, people may wish us harm. There is plenty of sad malice in the world, both obvious and quiet.

Second, and perhaps more likely, people are simply so caught up in their own needs that they are quite oblivious to yours. This is not malice - just the common or garden selfishness of the human animal.

The third possible reason is ignorance. These people do not know who you are, so how can they be expected to deliver what you need? The uncle who gave me the same chocolate bar for Christmas for thirty years had misunderstood polite noises when first offered for genuine appreciation. It was well-meaning ignorance but it was ignorance.

Love is the ability to stand in someone else's shoes, and feel their needs, but love is a rare commodity. Most advice is given to us by people standing firmly in their own shoes, and ignorant as to the shape of our heart. It is for reasons such as these that people cannot be trusted.

❋

In such a setting, trust is not a virtue to aspire to; not something we should be straining every fibre of our being to achieve. Trust is not an achievement but a gift - a gift bestowed on us by another.

We can relax in our efforts to trust, for trust is not something we do, but something done to us. When someone so graces our lives that we find ourselves trusting them, this is not something we have achieved for ourselves. Rather, the feeling of trust is created in us by another, whose trustworthiness gradually stains our soul in all its wonderful colours.

And so it is that if someone trusts you, it is not because they are good - but because you are good; because something in you has created that possibility in them. For those who struggle to see themselves as good, this may be hard to believe - but it is true.

If trust is not created within you easily, it suggests that you were born into the sustained practice of ignorance concerning your needs. This is not to condemn those who nurtured us. If I say that a play was poor, I am not condemning the playwright - just commenting on a piece of their work. We each fail on many levels constantly, both knowingly and unknowingly. To reflect truthfully on our nurturing is merely to tell it as it is, for these are things we need to know, that we might travel more joyfully.

Parents cannot give to another what they do not themselves possess, and as most parents are ignorant of their own selves, they will have difficulty in seeing and nurturing the self in another. As the child looked to them in trust, hoping to have mirrored back something supportive of its identity, they may well have been disappointed by the ignorance and selfishness of the carer, just as the carer was by their own parents, all those years before. Sadly, however, they have chosen to remain in the vicious circle. Instead facing the ignorant damage done to them, they deny its existence and lazily pass it on to their child. An unconscious soul cannot in itself nurture consciousness; just as the ignorant soul cannot mirror understanding.

If we do not trust someone, it is probably because they have not created that possibility within us.

*

An impoverished sense of identity is common enough and it is a dangerous lack in our psychological make-up. People with such a condition will be familiar to us, recognized in such traits as an insatiable need and demand for support; in an overbearing or inappropriately grand sense of themselves; in a relentless craving for admiration, approval and attention, combined with a lack of empathy for others and lack of interest in their concerns. By their fruits you will recognize them - and perhaps weep for their past.

*

Families wield huge power. In the face of disapproval and disbelief, we can easily wilt and drift into a life that is less than we might have lived. Perhaps we wonder endlessly if we are doing the right thing or what others might think or if perhaps we should try something else. Yet we are hesitant to risk anything, fearing we might fail or concerned that others might laugh or criticize.

It is important to remind ourselves in such circumstances that these were not fears or concerns we possessed when we were born. To this extent, they are not who we are, but an alien hand scrawled across our lives. When we were born, we belonged completely to the world and the world belonged completely to us; and this remains our true self. These fears and worries were placed in us by our upbringing, and the quicker we bid them farewell and return to our true selves, the better.

Returning to the incident between Jesus and his brothers, we discover that blood is not always thicker than water. Many people had found something in Jesus, but his brothers were not among them. It was not in Jesus' power to change things at that time, and he could only live the present. So he accepts their ignorance, not as the ultimate truth of how things are, but as the way of the current unfolding. He will neither collude with their ignorance nor flatter it with polite words of friendship; but neither will he waste his time in debating the matter.

He neither complained or explained. Instead, he withdrew from them, and stayed for a while in Galilee, to mind his inner fire, for sometimes it seemed that fire was all he had. Later, when he judged the time to be right, he went to the festival alone, without his family. For the moment, this was the perfect way.

*

It is strange how families don't know each other very well.

Asking someone to describe a member of their family is often an unrevealing experience, as any priest will tell you, who has sat with relatives preparing for the funeral of a loved one lost. Often, it is akin to asking a fish to describe water. It is difficult when you have always known someone, when they have been part of your formation. After all, they helped create the eyes with which you now look at them. In such a situation, how can we possibly view anyone accurately? People can describe a person they met for ten minutes at a bus stop. But as for describing their deceased brother Kevin? 'Well, he was Kevin, wasn't he? I mean, what else can you say? Kevin was Kevin. And we'll miss him. Of course we will.'

You want to know so many things about Kevin. What made Kevin cry, for instance? Or what made Kevin's heart sing? What nightmares fractured his sleep? What lifted his eyes to the heavens in thanks? So much to know! Yet often, these are not things families do know. They know Kevin liked a drink or an occasional flutter on the horses, or that he was a bit of a joker, and spent Wednesday at the allotment, but they do not know the hidden things which underscored his life. These are often not matters which families deal in.

One of the dangers of such family ignorance is that we can quietly and unknowingly absorb it and, almost without realizing it, join them there, knowing ourselves only in the superficial things. Their lack of knowledge concerning us can silently become ours. If our family decides for us a role - Kevin was the joker, for instance - it is very hard not to believe that role to be defining of who we are. There is the famous story of the eagle who thought she was a farmyard chicken. Surrounded by chickens all her life, having been born in a farmyard, the eagle never thought she was anything other than one of them.

Sometimes she would look in the sky and see the eagles flying high on the wind, elegant and fine, but the creatures around her kept saying that she was wasting her time, since she was a farmyard chicken, and she best get used to it. They were trying to be kind in their own depressed sort of way. It was just that they were wrong, as family often is. And there was a lot more to Kevin than merely being the joker.

And I am put in mind of St Francis of Assisi, generally thought to be one of the finer men to grace this earth. But was his father proud of him? No. St Francis in fact was a severe disappointment to his father, who was a successful merchant and sensibly wished likewise for his son, as any parent would. From where he was standing, this was love - to give his son the same opportunities that he had. Doesn't any parent want the best for their child? An unemployed saint might look good from a distance, but from the family perspective, it was just embarrassing.

From a place of ignorance, this Italian businessman was offering what he believed to be love and reckoned to be wisdom, but would young Francis listen? Well, he probably did listen, but he did not agree. Discerning from an inner place the nature of his father's aspirations for him, Francis, like Jesus with his brothers, set off in the opposite direction to the one suggested. And thus it was amid family hostility that he took the first tentative steps towards genuine adventure.

Families can be savage to those who do not fulfil their obligations. The feeling is that they brought you up, they put up with you, they invested in you and now you owe them something; the feeling is that after all they've done for you, anything else but compliance on your part is ingratitude.

The family will protect you as long as you toe the line, because that's what families are for, to look after their own. But step out of line and you will feel the heat, as one flying too close to the sun.

*

Your teaching as a child was placed in the wrong hands, of course; for your teacher was a fraud. Adults cannot teach children.

Family learning is generally based on the assumption that the adult knows more than the child, and is therefore fit to instruct. And they are deemed fit to instruct because they are older in years, and have experience of the world. They must know the score, surely? Well, this would be wonderful if it were so, but clearly it isn't.

Parents do not know the score. Indeed, the opposite is true, with the child knowing many profound things with which the adult has lost touch. The child, for instance, lives only from its adventuring soul, wide open to all things, whereas the adult lives from the cramped confines of the false personality it has created over the years in order to protect itself. The adventuring soul is the glory, and the false personality the nightmare.

But the nightmare is boss. And so it is that we have the situation where wise children are brought up by foolish adults, and quickly learn their ways.

Here is a story: The little girl is fascinated. She is watching this amazing, colourful and fluttering miracle. She chases it, shrieking delight and wonder. Her dad, sensing an educational opportunity, grabs her by the arm, stopping her gleeful chase in its tracks. 'That's a butterfly, darling,' he says firmly and spells the word for her. He makes her repeat it after him, ten times.

And she learns well, the little girl, for next time she sees it, she doesn't shriek in pleasure at the fluttering miracle, for she sees no miracle - just a butterfly. 'That's a butterfly,' she says to her dad, making sure to pronounce it right, and her dad is very pleased at her progress - able to categorize nature and only eight years old! Marvellous. And she also feels good that now she knows the sort of thing that pleases her dad. She must do more things like that.

Soon she will be as emotionally and spiritually dead as her father.

Perhaps you feel we should have more sympathy for the father in this story, for he is surely a victim too? After all, the words he speaks are not the words of his true self, but alien words, scorched into his vulnerable soul when young. He can't help behaving as he does, for it is all he knows. You can't speak from what you haven't discovered. As far as he's concerned, he's just doing his best amid the bleak wreckage of his own inner life.

These things are true, and as a victim, he has my sympathies. Unfortunately, however, he has now joined the sad company of the vicious circle. He too has become a perpetrator, and we cannot either applaud or support him in that. The morally lazy or psychologically unaware victim always becomes the perpetrator. Because they do not sift through the rubble of their past, and face that which must be faced, they tend to perpetuate the misdemeanours of their parents or carers.

I am not concerned here with condemnation of such people, for I hear the crucified words. When Jesus was hanging on the cross he spoke some remarkable words about those who had worked so hard and so calculatingly to nail him there: 'Forgive them, father, for they know not what they do.'

These words hover like a mist of mercy above our planet, and are the backdrop to all these reflections. None of us truly know what we do, for if we did, we would instantly die of shame.

But this also is true: that when people brought their children to Jesus, that he might bless them, the disciples played the big-bodied-adult card. Seeing the little legs journeying towards Jesus, they intervened to stop the children from wasting the teacher's time. Jesus firmly rebuked the disciples' mistaken consciences.

We will not be hard on the disciples. They had probably not been valued as children when they were young, so could not imagine why these children should be valued now. Jesus, however, thought otherwise: 'Let the children come to me and do not stop them, because the kingdom of God belongs to such as these.'

Children apparently know more than adults, in the areas that count. Children instinctively understand that they are beginners; that they are at the beginning of their lives. They know nothing about anything, they are innocents and have everything to discover. And so it is for us. We are invited by Jesus to achieve again this same innocence, this embarrassing lack of sophistication, which creates the possibility of revelation. We must resolve always to be beginning, always to be starting out - for the kingdom of God belongs to such as these.

And so it is that dire warnings are given by Jesus to any who attempt to lead the young astray; any who attempt to turn absolute beginners into those who have absolutely nothing to learn. Forgiveness may be the ultimate gift to such people; nothing is impossible. But we will not collude with their death-bringing activity along the way.

*

The world would be a different place if the older one got, the wiser one became, but experience points to the truth that age and wisdom are not related. As Jesus has suggested, children know more than adults in the areas that count, with a natural understanding of, and openness towards, the kingdom of God. So contrary to the familiar saying that 'father knows best', father may well not know best; indeed, father may very well merely be passing on the brand of ignorance originally delivered to him. It is as though he was given a sealed letter which he has trusted and believed in, but never actually opened or examined.

And now here he is, passing it on to you, still oblivious to its contents, but wanting you to have it nonetheless.

The expectation is that you will not read it either, but faithfully pass it on in turn to your children. He was not curious to understand anything inside the envelope, and you need not be either. The sealed letter gets passed on and on and on, down the generations.

Once we see that most humans only grow in a technical sense; once we stop respecting age for age's sake, then we become much freer souls in our relationships with them. We no longer idealize them in any manner, or attribute wisdom where it doesn't exist, but see them simply for who they are.

Meet the proud dad with his first child. There he is, holding the little life in his strong arms, and of course he is as pleased as a very pleased Mr Punch. Who knows? Perhaps she will grow up to be a daddy's girl! He would like that. But we do not look at her for the moment, in all her unknowing, but at the man holding her. What can we say of the large person to whom the tiny body of the child clings? Surely he is the one who knows everything and the child nothing? Well, he may know more facts than when he was young - but sadly, both for him and his daughter, he probably knows less glory.

Granted, he has acquired a lot of information down the years. When he was born, he didn't know the capital of Brazil, for instance, or how to change a light bulb or when to lift the foot from the clutch when changing gear in the car, and he knows all those things now. He can talk about mortgages, is an avid reader of the papers, particularly the stocks and shares pages, and organizes work outings to France. What more could you ask? He knows what he likes, likes what he knows, cooks a fine barbecue, has strong views on a wide range of subjects, so here is a man of the world, surely? Here is a man to teach his child well.

But we should never mistake the acquisition of information for personal growth; we should never mistake information for truth. We may live on a super information highway, but it apparently makes no difference to the way we behave, which is neither super, informed nor a highway that is going anywhere other than in circles.

So the man holding the child has grown in a technical sense, but shrunk in an emotional sense. The fact is that when he was born, he was altogether bigger than this. As a tiny baby, he was a vast hallway of sunlit and fluid openness to the mystery world. Now, he is a narrow corridor of cramped and hardening opinion. This is not glory. This man may appear to be what society regards as a good father, but he can teach his child nothing of lasting worth and the best the child can hope for is that she will appreciate this as soon as possible, and find her own inner fire to light and warm her journey. As Blake said, 'The eagle never lost so much time as when he submitted to learn from the crow.'

*

The role of the enlightened witness in the health of a child is most crucial; someone outside the immediate family set-up, with whom we can talk about our feelings. They do not need us to be anything other than what we are. If this figure has existed, perhaps in a grandparent or family friend or youth leader or meal supervisor at school, then it is possible for the adult to come to be a witness to their childhood in a most helpful manner. Returning for a moment to Amelia's childhood, we remember that in the face of an aggressive father, and passive mother, she always had her nan. It wasn't that they talked about her family life. It was simply that Amelia experienced there a different quality of relationship which, even as a child, will have helped her appreciate that there was a world beyond her home life.

Her nan helped her stand outside her family as an observer, and this would aid her considerably in her later years. Her nan had provided a crack of light in the darkness. Her nan had given her the belief that she was worthy of love, something which her home had not given her. If someone knows they are worthy of love, then there are good chances for healing in the later years. And when her nan died, Amelia knew it was time to face things herself. It was time for the crack of light to become a flood.

If we were not fortunate enough to have such a witness, then we will have had to find other ways to survive. Without anywhere we could express our feelings, we had to bury them. Feelings which needed to be spoken and felt were denied. They were put in cod storage where they have sat, waiting. Those without a witness will enter adult life with all sorts of unexamined leftovers from childhood, frozen deep within. And this desperate material will do its work from the unseen places, which perhaps do the worst work of all.

And here we could listen to the story of Sandy, in which we witness the consequences of a child burying feelings she cannot face.

Sandy is threatening to walk out on Bob, who she loves. And before you jump to any conclusions, it isn't about another woman. Sandy and Bob are a second family, with Bob having access to his two boys from his first marriage every weekend. The boys are polite to Sandy when they come round, but she just can't bear them being about the place, making a noise and taking all of Bob's attention. She sometimes feels he prefers them to her, and now she has reached the stage where it is either them who go, or her.

Sandy is going to let Bob make up his own mind, but she is fearful of the outcome. She doesn't know how it has come to this, for the boys have been as good as they could be, and she knows Bob is being a good dad, just as she would wish him to be. But for some reason, the situation is intolerable for her. Perhaps she is going mad.

What Sandy is presently unaware of is that this is an exact repeat of tragic family dynamics from her past, when the man she adored most, her father, had constantly seemed to be with her two brothers, and therefore unavailable to her. She could not allow herself to feel this rejection, and so it was buried in order that she might survive. Now, however, Bob and his two boys were touching the nerve, whose roots went way back into her past and the pain was quite impossible, forcing her to threaten to leave that which she most wanted.

If she could make the connection to her past, then there could be a way back home. But with no witness to her feelings in childhood, no kind light in her pain, they were understandably buried very deep. Certainly her family would not be able to help her in this matter.

In the legal world, ignorance of the law is not a defence, and may well lead to harsh penalties. In the emotional world, the penalties for ignorance of our past - ignorance of who we are, and why we are - are perhaps greater still. There is no way back while our feelings are blocked, and the ubiquitous blindness of those who do not understand their feelings is perhaps what most threatens life on this planet.

*

Those who repress feelings also hurt themselves. Finally science has caught up with ancient wisdom, and is now aware of the intimate relationship between emotion and body; and of the extraordinary biological intelligence which is the human. My body is not merely a machine controlled by my brain, via appropriate electrical impulses. Rather, I am a psychosomatic miracle, my cells communicating with each other, adjusting and changing according to need. As Aristotle is supposed to have said, 'Soul and body, I suggest, react sympathetically upon each other.' His observations on the natural world were not always on the mark, but this one certainly was.

We take part in our own health with the decisions we take. When emotions are expressed, and the bio-chemicals which are the physical expression of emotion flow freely through us, then our body system is united and whole. But when emotions are not expressed or denied, then the intricate network of inner pathways is blocked, and energy for health stymied. The unifying chemicals which organize our body and behaviour are blocked from their beautiful business and our physical body becomes part of a dangerous and distorting subconscious, the dumping ground of unexpressed feeling.

*

It is time to wind up this section, but perhaps we have glimpsed that families can, knowingly or unwittingly, become a conspiracy against growing up. Perhaps they fear that our growing up is also growing different. While families might allow us to age, they might be less willing to allow us to mature, since our maturity might threaten the fragile balance of things. You have been given a role to play. If you decide to change that role, it could end up upsetting everyone.

The story is told of a man who meets someone in the street. He is greeted warmly by them: 'Barry! Good to see you, but how you've changed! You used to be so tall and now you're so short! And you used to be so thin and now you're so fat! And you used to have blond curly hair and now it's dark and straight!' 'My name's not Barry. It's Wayne,' replies the other. 'What?! You've changed your name as well?!'

It is not only strangers who don't know who we are, but are determined to assume endlessly.

Jesus' role, chosen independently of his disapproving family, certainly upset the assumptions of his brothers. Whether they knew what they wanted, we don't know, but they certainly knew what they didn't want. It was a family conspiracy of ignorance - and so Jesus went to the festival alone.

The murder of family

Meet Rosemary. She is hunting for a Mother's Day card, as society says she should. If you can't send a card and some flowers to your mother once a year, then what are you?! The shop is full to bursting with sentimental verse and rose-coloured cards, which for some reason Rosemary struggles with. But even as she thinks it, she punishes herself for having such feelings. Everyone should be devoted to their mother in Rosemary's view, and everyone should be loyal, because if you cannot pledge loyalty to your mum, you must be the lowest of the low.

Rosemary's eating problems are a cause of profound unhappiness to her, but what can she change? She must put aside such thoughts and find a nice card.

We should not mistake loyalty for love in this story, though Rosemary did. From infancy, she had drunk in the negativity of her mother towards her, but was determined to love the person who was destroying her. The evidence for her love for her mother was her hatred of herself. She must love her mother more, and if that meant hating herself more, then so be it.

In Rosemary's view, it is wrong to be disloyal to family and right to go to the card shop. But in this incident, Jesus takes a different approach.

Jesus was still talking to the people when his mother and brothers arrived. They stood outside, asking to speak with him. So one of the people there said to him, 'Look, your mother and brothers are standing outside, and they want to speak with you.' Jesus answered, 'Who is my mother? Who are my brothers?' Then he pointed to his disciples and said, 'Look! Here are my mother and my brothers! Whoever does what my father in heaven wants him to do is my brother, my sister, and my mother.' Matthew 12.46-50

Matthew, Mark and Luke all record this remarkable incident in which Jesus disowns his mother and the rest of his family. And as we contemplate the words, it is hard to know which is the more remarkable: the sheer offensiveness of the remarks or the degree to which they have been completely ignored ever since. But the fact is that in 34 words, Jesus undercuts lineage as the determining factor in family, and drives a coach and horses through the assumption of parental authority. On the face of it, it is hard to see what more he could have done or said to dismantle all traditional notions of family; not to mention the personal offence he must have caused his mother, brothers and sisters.

When you visit your offspring at work on the off-chance they are free, it might well be that you find they are caught up in a meeting or busy on the till with a long queue to deal with or out visiting a client or handling a large delivery of tulips from Holland. But you can at least expect that if you leave a message, they will get back to you with a time when they will be free. It is the least they can do for the one who brought them into the world, surely?

Jesus, however, doesn't offer his mother a time when he is free. Instead, he tells her that he is with his family already; family as in 'people he feels an affinity with'. The conversation among his distraught relations as they left that place will not have been cheery or full of good will towards the eldest son. They had feared Jesus was losing the plot, had told him so often - and this merely will have confirmed it. 'Who is my mother?' indeed! They will never have heard such rudeness! And frankly, what sort of an example to the listening crowd was behaviour like this? After all, they all had families. Jesus should be teaching respect.

*

This harsh scene did not arise out of nowhere. Everything has a context, and as we are aware, there was a history of tension in the holy family. In particular, there was a history of negativity towards Jesus' chosen path.

Drawing on past experiences, Jesus sensed the reason for their visit and had no desire to collude in this manipulative action. And so he cuts the legs from beneath the grounds of their plea. 'We are family,' they say, you should listen to us!' 'You are not my family,' he replies, and looking out at the faces of the searching before him, he simply says, 'This is my family.'

In some cultures, parents and grandparents have authority merely because of the position they hold in the family hierarchy. They are to be respected because of their age and their status. What they are inside is not considered a significant factor in the matter. They are to be treated with respect whatever. In other cultures, greater attachment is placed on emotional feelings towards parents. The general message is that you should love your parents, be nice to them, visit them often and celebrate Mother's Day and Father's Day, as the card industry links eager hands with sentimentality.

Jesus did not noticeably adopt either of these approaches. These 34 words are disturbing things to say in any culture, but Jesus' own culture would have been one particularly threatened by such remarks. The Greek word used here for family, *patria* is primarily concerned with lineage or descent, providing the historical origin of a household, and therefore its identity. With lineage so fundamental in a patriarchal society, the original patriarch of the family would often have been more esteemed than the present master of the house. In this understanding, 'family' might be used not just to describe a household, but could refer also to a tribe or even a nation, which found its identity in origins of shared blood.

But Jesus does not identify with the loyalty of shared blood, and in doing so, undermines the careful authority structure of the household. It was a power structure built on direct descent from the original patriarch and the consequent status this bestowed on significant family members. But Jesus simply does not accept this hierarchy. If he can ask, 'Who is my mother?' then he could also ask, 'Who is my father?' which in his society went to the very heart of authority and identity.

And while the early Church gave us these surprising Gospel stories, it must have done so in trepidation. The early church depended on the household as a unit for its own growth and stability. Already among the Jews, the household was the primary context in which the faith was passed on through the weekly celebration of sacred meals, family prayers and religious instruction. Christian families would have adopted this model also and in the Jerusalem church in the early days, the Eucharist took place by households. They really couldn't have people overthrowing this model.

Thus, the household mattered both in society and in the Church in first-century Palestine, and the household was founded on lineage and the authority that bestowed. Only a madman would question such things. No wonder Jesus was ignored. Reported, but ignored.

*

It must have been tempting to censor some incidents in the Gospels, and I can imagine few more in danger of ending up on the cutting room floor than the one we consider here.

Look at it from the perspective of the religious hierarchy. It is an unexploded bomb on their doorstep. People disowning their parents willy-nilly? It didn't bear thinking about. I can see a committee being formed to decide whether it stays in the Gospels or is removed. I can see them gathering on the day of their meeting and chatting among themselves, catching up on news; I can see the latecomers rushing to grab a coffee and biscuit, and I can hear the words of the chairman as he opens the proceedings:

'Welcome, everybody. Thank you for coming today. I hope you all signed in at reception, found your name badges and refreshments. It's a while till lunch and we have a full agenda. The toilets, by the way, if you haven't found them already, are on the left hand side down the corridor.

But now, getting straight down to business, we have an important matter to discuss. As I am sure you're only too well aware, for the sake of ourselves and posterity, we need to come to a decision about these rather troublesome words of Jesus concerning his family, mentioned in the briefing document. What precisely is their value? And if they have value, does it outweigh some of the more worrying implications of these ideas being put in the public domain. By the time we leave today, one thing is certain: we must have decided whether they are in or out.

So let us start with the obvious. These words undoubtedly fly in the face of our current social structure, and in particular, the fifth Commandment's time-honoured words about honouring your mother and father. There is scant honour on display here! We have always felt that wonderful law to be written in stone and therefore untouchable. Until now, of course. Not a dull moment with Jesus around, bless him! Says he supports the law, he always said that, but frankly, I do wonder sometimes.

Speaking off the record, I probably wish that these words had not been spoken at all. There, I've said it! Well, I mean, they certainly don't make our lives as religious leaders any easier, do they? And it is not as if we don't have enough problems with discipline already. But the hard fact is that they have been spoken, and spoken by Jesus our Lord, and we need to jump one way or the other.

Now obviously to some degree the words can be put in perspective. Jesus was the Messiah after all, so allowances can be made. Messiahs can perhaps break a few rules which us lesser mortals have to stick to. Yes - it might make it a good deal easier for everyone concerned if messiahs didn't break the rules, but we can't do anything about that. We just have to pick up the pieces and make the best of things.

So yes, these are words which can, to some extent, be put into perspective, and therefore their impact diluted. We put it like this: 'These words were said by the Messiah in relation to his particular family - but that doesn't mean we can say them about our families! He was the Messiah, chummy - we're not!' That could be our take on it.

So one option is that we go ahead and publish them as words of his, but that we don't in any manner recommend them as guiding words for the general public. We surround them with moral warnings, making very clear that just because it was all right for Jesus, doesn't make it all right for us. As I say, we put the words in perspective.

The other option is that we don't publish these words at all, on the grounds that they are just too dangerous. Certainly no government could ever be seen to be backing such sentiments, both for the bad publicity that would fall on their heads - they all want to be the 'family values' party after all - and for the fact that the family is such a key social and economic unit.

Obviously we are not ruled by the public reaction to what we do, God forbid! But it is prudent not to fall out with the world, and in particular the press, who are best kept as close as possible. To fall out with them over a time-honoured institution such as the family does smell of madness. With the power of edit, they can make you look very stupid, and I for one can do without that sort of crucifixion.

And then we also have pastoral responsibilities here. I say people are just not ready to hear the things which Jesus is saying, not ready for that sort of freedom. People need the bedrock of their parents. Take that away and they will be all over the place! Family is family after all. 'Uncage the home bird, and it will die in the wild,' as the ancients say. We have to be very aware of the psychological consequences of our decision here.'

Which way would the vote go at the end of the day? I imagine it endorsing censorship, perhaps by four votes to one. Fortunately for us, however, the Gospel writers threw all that caution to the winds and simply told the story as it was.

*

I can remember taking part in the beautiful Christmas liturgies. Some would then leave with joyful step for an eagerly anticipated time with their relations over the festive season. It was for them a good time, a time they looked forward to, past family Christmases still close to their hearts.

But there were many for whom this was not the case. As they left for the obligatory family Christmas, they could be recognized by their haunted eyes. They would say goodbye to each other as those going to war, and with all the joy of Captain Oates leaving the tent for the blizzard: 'I may be gone some time.'

Good people are often hurt by the destructive dynamics that come into play when families gather; they find themselves quite powerless to deal with them. They regress, become children again, and allow themselves to be defined by figures who loomed so large in their past. Each year they think that they can handle it. Each year they don't. Christmas, of course, has nothing to do with the family, but somehow we feel obliged each year to reinvent the myth, and place ourselves, for good or ill, in its power.

*

I remember a February walk, and there by the road, daffodils in the snow. I had to stop and stare, intrigued by the clashing messages, the various truths nestling up to each other, as winter and spring fought for the throne. They could not both win. The snow spoke of the persisting grip of the cold. The daffodils promised the arrival of the warm. If the cold managed one dying surge, the flower would be killed before its full bloom. But if the flower could survive another day or two, then the cold would be history, and the flower freed to live its springtime glory. It was a life and death struggle there by the road.

As I say, the standard line is that family, like sunlight or clean water, is assumed to be good. No one can question family; it is the bedrock of society. If you have a problem with it, then the problem is yours. And so instead of questioning the past, because that is not permitted, or evaluating the present, for that upsets the fragile apple cart of family dynamics, the crying inner child in each of us closes down to the truth trapped in our bodies and instead takes out our anger externally on everything and everyone else around us. We shout at our friend on the doorstep. Or we are cold to our colleague at work. We are resentful towards our children. We are negative towards that person with the new idea. Suddenly they are the enemy, as feelings well up inside us, like an inner volcanic surge. We are of course misplacing our frustration, but that is not going to stop us. It's easier than facing the truth of feelings long buried. Our behaviour is inappropriate, misguided and foolish. But it appears to be the only way. As with the daffodil in the snow, it is a life and death struggle.

*

Here is a family tale from the Bible, featuring Abraham, his son Isaac, God and an unfortunate ram who was in the wrong place at the wrong time.

Sometime later God tested Abraham; he called to him, 'Abraham!' And Abraham answered, 'Yes, here I am!' 'Take your son,' God said, 'your only son, Isaac, whom you love so much, and go to the land of Moriah. There on a mountain that I will show you, offer him as a sacrifice to me.' Early the next morning, Abraham cut some wood for the sacrifice, loaded his donkey, and took Isaac and two servants with him. They started out for the place that God had told him about. On the third day Abraham saw the place in the distance. Then he said to the servants, 'Stay here with the donkey. The boy and I will go over there and worship, and then we will come back to you.' Abraham made Isaac carry the wood for the sacrifice, and he himself carried a knife and live coals for starting the fire. As they walked along together, Isaac said, 'Father!' He answered, 'Yes, my son?' Isaac asked, 'I see that you have the coals and the wood, but where is the lamb for the sacrifice?' Abraham answered, 'God himself will provide one.' And the two of them walked on together.

When they came to the place which God had told him about, Abraham built an altar and arranged the wood on it. He tied up his son and placed him on the altar, on top of the wood. Then he picked up the knife to kill him.

Genesis 22.1-10

An angel then intervenes and tells Abraham not to hurt the boy, that he has passed the test of faith, showing himself fully prepared to kill even his son if asked. A ram caught in a bush by its horns is killed instead. And father and son make their way home.

*

I have always found this a repulsive story. There has never been any sense of peace or goodness attached to it; nothing admirable to wonder at, though in my younger days, it might have been hard to tell you why I wanted to turn the page quite so fast. Perhaps even then, however, I struggled with the feeling that however much you spiritualize or theologize the tale, it is hard to disguise the fact that the two supposed heroes - Abraham and God - collude together to torment a child terribly, and that the feelings of the child are completely ignored. These are serious offences.

The passing years and further reflection have not improved the picture. Here is a story of a father who quietly agrees to kill his son when asked by the Almighty. It is a story which includes a death march: the three-day walk of father and son, with the son being endlessly deceived about their destination and plans. As a parent I am repulsed by the idea, and as a child, I am terrified. A walk together is usually a trusting and close affair, but not here.

We then reach the awful moment which the storyteller, perhaps unsurprisingly, skims over, when Abraham finally turns towards his son, and using both his physical strength and the authority vested in him, forces his son to climb falteringly up onto the altar, and begins to tie him up with cord; it will need to be tight, otherwise his son might wriggle in an attempt to evade the plunging knife. How would you handle this if you were the parent, if you were Abraham?

There is no dialogue recorded for this part of the story. Is Isaac literally dumb-struck? Certainly he is still unknowing of the fate his father has planned, though he must be weeping inside with confusion and fear. Finally, the knife-holding hand of the adult is raised, and suddenly, the truth is very clear to young Isaac. His father, the man he trusts above all others, is about to kill him.

What is there to commend this story? If it was a story about the merits of blind obedience, then we might as well celebrate the blind obedience of the faithful souls who faithfully carried out their necessary tasks in the death camps of Auschwitz or Treblinka. What ethical check on obedience exists if child murder can be applauded when carried out obediently? And what of the feelings of the child? Do you ever recover from such an incident? Presumably your only path of survival is to deny within that it ever happened. 'My father would never have done that. I must be making it up.' How we react to this story will vary a great deal.

Different bells will be ringing in us depending on what histories and attitudes we bring to it. But it is perhaps a touchstone for us all on the subject of authority. When Alice Miller was looking at paintings of this story, to see what the episode had drawn from artists in the past, she noticed a number of interesting things. She noticed, for instance, that in all the paintings, Abraham's face, or even entire torso, is turned away from Isaac and looking heavenwards. Certainly it would have been hard to look Isaac in the eye at this time, and anyway, Abraham is busy with God; not with the feelings of his helpless child.

For the boy, that must have been the ultimate loneliness. He lies there in terrible danger, but his father, the man he respects and who he looks to for protection, chooses not to be there with him. His father is busy with someone else.

Something else which caught Alice Miller's eye was that Isaac is always passive in the paintings. In one picture, he has tears in his eyes, but there is no picture which depicts him as struggling or rebelling against his treatment.

The artists had clearly learned to be obedient children in all circumstances, and found no difficulty in portraying Isaac as an accepting victim, even in the face of his own murder. How else could such passivity flow from their skilled brushes which in other circumstances could portray overwhelming emotion? There in their own inner make-up was the belief that if God and your father wanted you murdered, then you should accept it in a dutiful and non-complaining manner. And so Isaac doesn't struggle and he doesn't ask why; instead, he lies hemmed in by a numbing inner wall of silence that ensures he does not go to forbidden places of questioning. Here is the picture of obedience; here is a 'good boy'.

It is significant that Jesus did not react in this way when he was murdered on a cross. In the unutterable bleakness of his situation, instead of gazing passively at the sky, in obedient submission to someone who must know better, he struggled to make any sense of it at all, screaming at his heavenly father, 'Why have you abandoned me?!' Isaac might well have asked the same of Abraham, but such honest and desperate words were not permitted to him, for that would have been to let his father down.

Jesus was different however: he challenged his family on earth and he challenged his father in heaven.

*

As we contemplate Jesus' murder of the family, there are certain aspects of it we will not mourn.

We will not, for instance, mourn the passing of family as institutionalized selfishness. It was an eighteenth-century Naskapi Native American who placed his finger accurately if painfully on this issue, when speaking with a French Jesuit who had come to teach him about morality. 'Thou hast no sense,' he said to the Jesuit. 'You French people love only your own children, but we love all the children of the tribe.'

We will not stay long with this simple observation, other than to say that when the impoverished and desperate egos of parents become embroiled in their own offspring, there develops an inappropriate form of attention offered to them. This can very easily pass for virtue in our society. Who would criticize someone for showering their child with the most expensive of material gifts? Or would criticize the mother for wanting her child to come first in her class? Or the father who can't imagine his child to be anything other than right when away from the home setting?

But attention such as this is not a virtuous attention. Rather, it is a clinging and controlling attention, the roots of which lie in unhealthy places. Such supposed generosity, such self-aggrandizing virtue, such ignorant support, grows out of nothing more beautiful than the lack of self-worth in the parents and the consequent desire to build a little empire of their own through their children. The world will not miss family as conceived in these terms.

*

This could be a difficult bit of the path through the woods of life. In the quest for what is ultimately true, we will suffer, for there can be no dismantling of foolishness without humiliation and despair. We will need to be brought to the end of our selves before true creation can begin. We will never seek out such pain, or wish it on ourselves, for we are fragile souls, with very little capacity for suffering or strength for true adventure. As strong pillars collapse around us, we must find new answers. But when dismantlement does knock on our door, we can never really be prepared.

We have created and live from little rat-runs of familiar activity, practice, attitude and belief. Within these safe passages, we feel in control. But there come moments when these pathways are blocked off, and what we thought was sorted isn't. Suddenly, we are numb with unknowing, desolate with no apparent pathway to follow. We are a fox at the end of the run.

I remember well the young mountaineer sitting in the hospital, paralysed from the waist down after a bad fall. She is 21, and she will never walk again. She will live her life in a wheelchair and she will always need help. This is not what this daring and independent young person imagined would be. She thought she knew what her future held, but now it is as if she knows nothing; as if she is starting all over again, but with neither map nor consolation. A grey wash of desolation colours her world; a choking anger at the loss of everything she ever wanted.

Can we feel any less angry at the dismantlement of family? Our small hopes die and our big hopes die, sometimes in unutterably savage ways, if they are hopes built on illusions. It is not that we have been bad people, for we are the best of people. It is just that we have been sold notions which are not sincere and not true. These include our notions of family. Jesus both lives and speaks opposition to traditional notions of family because, ultimately, they are not true, but an illusion from which we need to be free.

*

There is a level of truth to the family, as there is to all convention. Society cannot function without certain conventions. Conventions glue things together; conventions attempt to organize goodness, and make things work in a tolerably efficient manner. And so it is we create places to look after our money, or buildings in which to pray, or places to go when we are hurt, or groups to look after us as children. But conventions like banks, churches, hospitals or families have no life in themselves. They are the mere formalizing of confused entanglements of need and desire, and they can as quickly become unhealthy places as wholesome places.

Unless we opt for life in a cave in a desert east of nowhere, we cannot avoid the conventions of public life and we will participate in them, sometimes very thankfully. But what we will not do is identify with them, for they simply do not exist in any very substantial sense.

They may have the appearance of enduring reality, but in truth, they have all the permanence of a stage set. In two hundred years' time, neither bank, church, hospital nor family will be there. We pass them as ships pass in the night. They are the briefest of conventions and designed to serve rather than be served.

And so it is that we shall sit light to them, celebrating their fleeting goodness certainly, but refusing to collude in their darkness and refusing to worship any claims to inherent authority.

*

For some, family members are treated as more than people. The family is a strange and compelling saga in which they are caught up, a drama which has an almost separate existence to normal life, and one which requires a different set of rules. Family worries for these people are not like normal worries, but have a unique power to unsettle. There are people. And then there is family.

For others, however, their family are less than people. Things done or not done in the past have created an almost total alienation. Parents refuse to acknowledge guilt. Children are cut off by their unresolved anger. There can be no return from this place. They will never speak again. It is over.

Both these attitudes, while making perfect sense to their adherents, are the foolishness of those still in the blind thrall of their conditioned psyche. They are living and acting from memory - as opposed to the present. But memory is stale; only the present is vital. They are as those who look out of their window seeking panoramic views, while at the same time keeping the blinds tight shut. They nail their feet to the floor and then try to hop, skip and jump.

When the blinds are opened and the nails removed; when the scales fall off our eyes and we see clearly beyond our conditioning, we no longer see family, but rather, we see people. We see individual people, alone in the world, making a fist of living, though not necessarily doing it very well. Most of the time they are unconscious of their motives and actions. They are sleep-walking their way through life because they fear what it would mean to wake up. In this, they are no different from anyone else.

They have no authority over you, no particular claim on you. They do not know themselves so how could they know you? And you do not know them, of course. Family are neither more than people, nor less than people. They are simply people.

True seeing cuts through the insubstantial mist of provisional forms, to the genuine worth of eternal forms. Family is provisional, people are eternal. It is better the family dies in us, in order that people might live in us.

*

Amid the ashes and collapse of everything we ever knew; amid the crucifixion of our cherished dreams; amid the numb silence of feelings frozen by fear, we will refuse to allow ourselves to be murdered; we will struggle to untie ourselves from the tight cords of convention, climb awkwardly down off the altar on which someone else placed us, stretch our cramped legs and step out into the future, to put life to the test, free of illusory entanglements. The family is dead. Now perhaps we can live.

The anointing of family

Meet Steve and Sadia. They are about to adopt a baby girl, who will be their first child. Soon they will meet with the foster mother, who has created a brief family for this baby. The foster mother is familiar with brief families, with being a safe place in hard times for little people. She loves them all, but soon she must let go and pass the child on into the hands of her new long-term family.

This will create a family of three who have come together through unwilled circumstances - but in great happiness at the outset of this adventure. The unwilled circumstances are the couple's inability to conceive a child of their own and the inability of the child's mother to raise her herself.

The happiness is in the union which has arisen out of the pain. And so a new family is born with the possibility of beauty, just as happened at the foot of the cross, when amid his crucifixion, Jesus gave Mary to John and John to Mary:

Standing close to Jesus' cross were his mother, his mother's sister, Mary the wife of Clopas, and Mary Magdalene.
Jesus saw his mother and the disciple he loved standing there; so he said to his mother, 'He is your son.' Then he said to the disciple, 'She is your mother.' From that time the disciple took her to live in his home.
John 19. 25-7 87

Once again, therefore, unwilled circumstances create a new family; one not of blood but of affinity and need.

Mary and John would certainly have known each other before this, and from Jesus' nailed perspective on the cross, they needed each other now. We do not know the network of relationships in which John and Mary were entwined at this time, but it certainly proved to be a significant moment for them both, for they shared a home from here on. This was perhaps not an outcome they imagined as they walked early up that skull-shaped hill, preparing themselves to face the worst, with nothing but emptiness in their souls and no sense of any possible future. Despair is the absence of possibility and that must have been their state as this day dawned. Jesus, however, creates possibility and on this occasion, it is possibility within a new family.

*

The words of Jesus from the cross echo down the centuries. This perhaps should not surprise, for the best of people in the worst of circumstances tend to find truth which enlightens others. Here are words spoken by a spiritual man amid suffering, a holy man holed, which creates a unique chemistry for truth, way beyond the reaches of the cheap convictions and second hand certainties that we are more familiar with from religious leaders.

When any of us encounter a level of experience which is beyond our normal knowing, there is a sudden sense of nakedness and exposure. We are like someone in a cold wind without the necessary clothes. In such situations, our traditional survival mechanisms are useless. The strengths we usually trade on are suddenly of no value at all. Jesus was pretty good with the sharp put-down, but that wasn't going to help him on the cross. He had a natural affinity with the suffering too, but he could hardly lay hands on anyone now. And he probably didn't feel like telling one of his clever little stories either. On the cross, he was taken beyond his gifts.

When we are taken to places beyond where we feel safe, we may look the same on the outside, but on the inside, we are the hollow people. It is like the first day at a new school. In our old school, we knew everything and everyone; we ruled the place. But suddenly, all that knowledge counts for nothing, for suddenly we are beginners again. You even have to ask directions for the toilets. The humiliation is profound.

When taken beyond our comfortable place, and exposed to a vulnerable place, there are two possible reactions. The first reaction is rooted in fear, and tends to the soul's hardening and shrivelling. The second reaction is rooted in openness, and tends towards the soul's recovery.

Fear is rigid, against life and leads us either into paralysis or to lashing out. Openness, on the other hand, creates the space in us to feel the new questions being asked, and to react spontaneously to them in fluid engagement with the world. For those who are open, 'the zero hour creates new algebras'.

Jesus lived predominantly from the second of these two places, that of openness to the unfolding of life. Amid the savage dismantling of the cross, he spoke new things from a new place. New settings create new words in him and us. Here he both speaks and enacts something new with family.

*

'Who is my mother?' Jesus once asked. He could at that time no longer tolerate the misuse of that role, which was making inappropriate claims on his life. But life is change, and the fire we contemplate in the hearth never twice looks the same; blink, and it is different.

Things are now different for Jesus, and whatever had happened in the past between them, his mother was now a person in need, a weeping soul, helpless to help him in his hour of greatest need. It is a strange place for the dove of possibility to be hovering, a place of such pain and fracture, but how good it is there, seeing all things, willing all things, creating all things. Jesus reaches out in spontaneous creation: 'Mary here is your son, and John, here is your mother.'

Spontaneity is the virtue of the open; of those escaping the predictable tramlines of automatic reaction and preset response; of those fluid amid present possibilities, and happy to know nothing of the future, save that it will be different from the past. There is no habitual way. There is only the constant recreation of oneself, through that which is encountered. Whatever Jesus had once wished for his family, it probably was not this remarkable twist of events, this strange blending of blood and affinity. But it happens nonetheless. Open to the future, in the painful now, Jesus anoints a new family and blesses a new household in perhaps his final earth-bound miracle.

*

It is interesting to note who stood with Jesus in his final hours. It was not a large crowd who gathered to say goodbye to him. Apart from John, none of his disciples felt able to be there, nor any of his brothers or sisters.

They all chose to miss the funeral. In fact, amid fears of further reprisals against associates of Jesus, attendance at the foot of the cross could be said to have sorted out the men from the boys, and on this occasion, three of the men were women. There were, it seems, two members of Jesus' blood family present, his mother and his aunt. The third figure standing watching was Jesus' best male friend, John, while the fourth was perhaps the most intriguing member of Jesus' family of affinity, Mary Magdalene. The very name conjures up all sorts of images, so maybe a brief portrait of this relationship would help.

Donatello's statue of Mary Magdalene is of a strong woman, but a woman battered by a harsh world, thin-faced and rough-haired, beseeching and broken, tough but humbled by her pain. And with the evidence before us, it is hard not to believe that this woman was Jesus' closest friend on earth.

They met when he cast seven demons out of her. We hear in Luke's Gospel of other women around Jesus. There was Joanna, whose husband Chuza was an officer in Herod's court, Susanna and many other women who used their own resources to help Jesus and his disciples. Here we have a little glimpse of Jesus' other family, a holy family of women, who were clearly at the heartbeat of the adventure. But it is the figure of Mary Magdalene who looms largest and loveliest in the life of Jesus. She was the woman who was there at the crucifixion, part of the select of group around the cross; and perhaps even more tellingly, she was the first person to whom the risen Christ appeared, in a haunting and wonderful anointing of the family of affinity.

Let us briefly relive the scene of encounter. Jesus has been killed. Mary Magdalene has gone to the tomb to oil the dead body. She finds the stone rolled away, and runs of to tell the disciples. Peter and John jump up and race each other to the tomb, but John is younger and wins the race rather easily, as he himself mentions. This shows that even the top disciples need affirmation occasionally and if others don't provide it then they must provide it themselves.

John and Peter both go inside the tomb, but find nothing apart from the linen wrappings of burial. They return home. Only Mary Magdalene now remains on this cold and joyless morning. Mary stands crying outside the tomb.

While she is still crying, she bends over and looks in the tomb and sees two angels dressed in white, sitting where the body of Jesus had been, one at the head and the other at the feet. 'Woman, why are you crying?' they ask her.

She answers, 'They have taken my Lord away and I do not know where they have put him!'

Then she turns round and sees Jesus standing there; but she does recognise him.

'Woman, why are you crying?' Jesus asks her. 'Who is it that you are looking for?'

She thinks he is the gardener, so she says to him, 'If you took him away, sir, tell me where you have put him, and I will go and get him.'

Jesus says to her, 'Mary!'

She turns towards him and says in Hebrew, 'Rabboni!' (This means 'Teacher'.)

'Do not hold on to me,' Jesus tells her, 'because I have not yet gone back up to the Father. But go to my brothers and tell them that I am returning to him who is my Father and their Father, my God and their God.'

So Mary Magdalene goes and tells the disciples that she had seen the Lord and relates to them what he had told her.

John 20.11-18

Let us state the obvious: to choose a woman as the first witness to an unlikely event is not a clever thing to do for a first-century Jewish writer seeking credibility. No writer would conceivably invent such a scenario as this.

If you were making it up, you would have a man as the key witness. Peter would have rushed into the tomb and discovered all - and sent Mary off on an errand to tell people about his discoveries. But it isn't like that. Peter goes home with John having found nothing, and it is to a woman that the epiphany is granted.

As I say, this would not be invented. So there is little doubt that Jesus chose to make his first resurrection appearance to Mary Magdalene, however much the early Church might have choked on the idea.

Why was Mary Magdalene chosen for such privilege? It was Heraclitus who said that a hidden connection is stronger than an obvious one, and my sense is that there is something of that here. She wasn't a disciple, she wasn't blood family, she had no official status in the entourage around Jesus. But apparently, she made Jesus' heart sing.

It is unsurprising that Mary Magdalene has excited so many imaginings, both historical and literary. Her life is open season for those who like to fill in the gaps, for there are many gaps to fill.

Gap-filling is not my task here; rather I wish only to reflect on the information before us. We don't have much by way of material concerning Jesus' life: just a few grainy photos from which to conjecture. But what seems clear from the body language of the snapshots on the table before us, concerning the relationship between Jesus and Mary, is that we are here looking at a special relationship.

The evidence is all towards a special friendship between two people and one which literally transcended death. What this friendship contained we do not know precisely. But such friendships have common roots. They arise from a shared place of utter safety, holding and pleasure; a gentle place where both can go when all around is collapsing, and find a brief healing for the soul; a place of honesty where even doubts about each other can be voiced, heard and held; a place where all things can be spoken, confusion acknowledged and the hurt bathed in something cool; a place of fragile but enduring union.

That Jesus and Mary Magdalene knew something of such a place seems likely, and my only reaction to such reflections is gladness - gladness that our Lord knew such friendship. To be a friend to everyone in the world, it helps to know friendship with one in the world.

We need not struggle to know more. We can celebrate the friendship and move joyfully on, for whatever hidden connection did lie between them, though it may have troubled the Church, clearly did not trouble Jesus. For Jesus, Mary, from Magdala, was family - perhaps the last face he saw before he died and certainly the first face he sought after his resurrection.

*

It is interesting to reflect on the four or five people we would want at the foot of the cross on which we were hanging. Are they the same people as those you might have named ten years ago or twenty years ago? It is one way into defining our current family.

And if you rose from the dead, who would be the first person you would seek out? Whose face would you most like to see? Who is the one most likely to celebrate your good news with you? Who would you like to hug and say, 'It's me!'

*

To return to the cheery song with which we started, both Mary, the mother of Jesus, and John are here invited to consider themselves at home, consider themselves one of the family - but a new family, related to the past, yet not the same as the past. Families evolve amid the flux of life, sometimes expanding, sometimes contracting, but never static. They live and change amid forces at work both within the individuals and the world. The family which Oliver joined in London in Dickens' classic tale became his refuge because of previous disappointment.

Unhappiness had driven him from his first home, so it was unwilled circumstance that brought him to his new family, just as it was for John and Mary at the foot of the cross. In Dickens' story, they proved to be a foster family for Oliver, until something more permanent emerged; though in truth, nothing is permanent in family, for nothing is permanent in life. The story is never over for anyone.

*

And of course Jesus' family story was not yet over either. We might have thought his words to his mother on the cross were his final family words, but it is very probable that they were not. Certainly we enter into murky historical territory here, with pitifully few facts to rub together into a coherent narrative. But we need not let that stymie us, for although we cannot be sure how things happened, we can be very sure that certain things did happen. We are weak on cause here, but strong on outcome, which is not an unfamiliar place to be. I do not need to know how the sun interacts with the earth, to enjoy a sunrise. It appears and I don't know how; it is enough for me that it does.

In like manner, we now witness another significant family reconciliation. How it happened we can only guess at; that something did happen is indisputable. As soon as the Gospel writers take up the story after the death of Jesus, it is clear that something has changed.

As Luke records early in the book of Acts, Jesus' family are suddenly identifying with him in a manner never seen during his brief life. After Jesus' ascension into heaven, his small band of followers met regularly, and Luke lists the apostles who were part of this group, but then adds the following: *They gathered frequently to pray as a group, together with the women and with Mary the mother of Jesus and with his brothers.*

Times change, people change, the previously impossible is suddenly normal and we do not always know why. For much of the time, we live amid what appears to be a fairly random chemistry of relationship in families. Things happen inside people, for good or ill, which we can barely guess at. We feel the effects of the inner change. But we do not know what caused them. In this instance, we know that a scene such as this before Jesus' death was not a possibility. The constant and at times bitter antagonism between Jesus and his family was old news. Yet here they are as followers.

What has happened? The most obvious conclusion, and one for which there is some primary evidence, is that one of the many appearances which Jesus made after his rising from the dead was to his blood family, and in particular, to his brother James. St Paul, writing a letter to the church in Corinth, gives a lead in the investigation, when he slips into his narrative, without any additional information, that Jesus appeared to 'James', and then to all the apostles. This could well be James, his brother. Certainly such a meeting is the best explanation of the sudden but sincere change in James towards Jesus - a change with visible and ultimately painful consequences. It was James, the formerly dismissive brother of Jesus, who became the first leader of the Christian Church in Jerusalem, the mother church of the world. Tradition then has it that he was martyred for his beliefs and leadership position. Josephus records him as being stoned, with other church leaders, around 62AD.

If this resurrection meeting between Jesus and James did take place, it must have been one of the most intriguing conversations of history. We will not demean it by trying to guess its content. Beauty is sometimes best left to the imagination, but the outcome was another anointing of family. During his life, Jesus never once colluded with the negativity of his brothers or his mother; never did he allow them to undermine his own self- understanding. Indeed, for much of his public life, he carried on despite his family, not because of them.

But neither, it seems, did he ever give up on them. Things would never return to how they had been. Family life cannot go backwards even if we were to wish it so; life is change. Instead, Jesus anoints new patterns and practice of family, good in new and unexpected ways. Released from the inappropriate power of family, Jesus returned to bless it, beyond its wildest dreams.

*

Family is an elastic concept both historically and presently. It does not describe any fixed model of relating - but rather, a human grouping of any sort in which there is connection by blood, affinity or even employment. The three are not mutually exclusive, of course. Shared blood does not preclude a huge and wonderful sense of affinity also. And while there was great affinity between Oliver and the other boys, they were still essentially a business, a team of pickpockets, employed for the profit of their master. Families come in all shapes, sizes and with significant fundraising potential.

81

*

But it is to contemplation we now return briefly, for amid such flux and variety of family life, it is the contemplative we celebrate, not the careless. To talk of shifting family patterns is not to baptize the actions of the careless or the destructive selfishness of the rootless soul, which neither knows what it wants nor cares what others want and who can prove so destructive to the fragile seeds of trust which family can nurture. We do not come to praise the careless, but the contemplative, who holds all things to the light and, like Jesus, destroys only that they might create.

Contemplation lies at the heart of the anointment of family, and we will now take a small step back from our subject to consider this most practical and helpful of activities; so useless yet so essential.

We start with a definition: Contemplation is separation leading to communion; the distinct experiencing no difference. What follows will seek to develop these ideas.

The first act of contemplation is the separation from the object being considered, in order to see that which we could not see. Let us take a walk to the edge of a lake, and watch the fish, as it swims around in the same manner as it has always done. It doesn't know either that it is a fish or that it lives in water. It has no sense of self, or understanding of its environment. It just is, in an unconscious sort of way.

Then one day it meets a flying fish who is unsettling initially, shooting up to the surface, disappearing for a moment into the unknown, before returning looking exhilarated. After a while, our nervous fish finally summons up the courage to follow him. He too shoots towards the surface and then suddenly, with a strong flick of his tail, he is - what's this?! He is a shape flying for a moment through non-water, before returning to the familiar deeps. What was that all about? All these years, he had thought he was water, but now he is shocked to discover that he still exists in non-water. He had seen himself, just for a moment, his gloriously colourful skin, brought to sparkling life in bright non-water. He wasn't water. He was a fish! There was so much happiness in that brief moment of separation from the water, as he experienced himself, and so much happiness as he plunged back into it, as he gloried in his homecoming.

For the first time, he appreciated the water, because he was not the water. He had always imagined they were one, and in a way they were, but you cannot be one, until you have become two. And you cannot bless the water, until you have left it.

We are separate people, and we can only experience our own consciousness. To this extent, we cannot know anybody else. The consciousness of others, of anyone who is not us, is a complete mystery. And therefore I separate not only to find out the shape of who I am, but also to live the truth that I cannot know you.

But this is not the end of the matter. For although I cannot know you, I can hold my experience of you in the gentle and considerate light of non-judgement. This does not come easily to us. Indeed, only the crucified can truly become contemplatives, for only the crucified can be hospitable to another within themselves. Having screamed at the darkening sky, and died to the conviction-fuelled ego, the contemplative now quietly tends the heart, watering it with their tears and finding that it becomes a place where others can live in peace - and find anointing.

In this manner we become one with those we hold in our hearts, as we experience distinction without difference. We may be separate from them, and certainly we cannot know them. But we are in some sense one with them. In a poem called 'The phoenix and the turtle,' Shakespeare expressed it like this:

So they lov'd as love in twain
Had the essence but in one
Two distincts, division none
Number there in love was slain.

Number is slain in this verse because as mathematicians and philosophers remind us, one is not in fact a number, but the ground from which all numbers spring. Mathematicians and philosophers here share the same truth as the contemplative, who also knows the ultimate purity and perfection of one; who knows that we are not merely one with our blood family or our family of affinity but with the human family.

Our true family is neither those caught up in the same little biological tangle as ourselves, or even those whose friendship we value - but the world. The world is our only true family, past, present and future. We share one heart beat and one God, and so with the biblical writer, we 'bow our knees before the father from whom every family in heaven and on earth is named'.

There is only one lineage, and that is the lineage of the divine glory existent and expressed in every human soul. Any understanding of family which is more exclusive than that, or smaller in scope than that, may have its moments of beauty and potential for delight, but remains always a contrivance of convention, a tiny piece of a vast jigsaw of unity and a pallid image of the ultimate and radiant truth that we are one.

✳

So number is slain, for we are one, distinct without difference. And it is from this place that we will create and live our brief families of blood, household and affinity.

We will neither raise them up too high in expectation, nor push them down too low in condemnation. We will not treat them as more than people. We will not bestow on our family any exclusive value, identify with them especially or allow them any power over us. Jesus invites us to leave behind the dismal and dangerous slavery of repressed feelings and inappropriate attachments.

But neither will we treat them as anything less than people, never imprison them in a box marked 'Finished with'. For people, unlike families, are eternal. And people are one. Such are the discoveries not of the careless but of the contemplative.

✳

Freud is not a name which excites universal applause, but then no name is worthy of universal applause. The best of us are granted to stumble upon the gift of partial truth, and in our better moments, find the courage and strength to live a little of it. Nevertheless, it was Freud who was instrumental in opening up a significant new vista of understanding and the vista was this: the human soul manages to survive its early traumas - profoundly terrible for one so psychically fragile and dependent as a small child - simply by avoiding awareness of them.

It's a simple but significant observation, for it's from the well of our past that we draw and drink for the rest of our lives. Is the water good? We peer down and can see nothing above the waterline. But it is what is below the waterline we should be concerned about, for it is that which seriously pollutes and beneath our waterline there is much.

There is no significant transformation for the human soul, until the polluted well of the past is dealt with. Neither a new bucket, improved pulley system, stronger rope or a complete repaint of the well's walls will make any difference at all. The water will still be undrinkable. We sometimes say to people 'What's done is done. Now let's move on.' But the repressed material within us will not allow this; fight it and there is only one winner, for it neither goes away of its own accord, nor can it be dismissed by our personal strength of will. It is not like dishwater, flushed easily down the plug hole, never to be seen again. Rather, it lodges obstinately within us, a parasite on our struggling beauty, in the nooks and crannies of our deep-down places. It patiently waits its turn, choosing its moments and all the while bleeding its pain quietly into our subconscious, staining it irrevocably. It is only a matter of time before our conscious self begins to be affected and before the death within plays out so tragically in our external lives.

Such insight as this did not exist in explicit form in either ancient wisdom or traditional religion. Certainly ancient teaching had been wise enough to observe that in its normal state, the human being is unconscious, or sleepwalking, or living in darkness. You can choose which description you like the best, but they all describe the same thing - disconnection with life. The link, however, between such insights as these and the terrified decisions taken by us when young, had not been made in the ancient teachings, and therefore they have struggled by themselves to offer liberation.

Ancient teachings have truthfully told me that I am unconscious, or sleep-walking or living in the dark. But they have not been able to tell me why I continue to choose such states, even when I am exposed for what I am. 'Choose freedom!' they tell me, to which we reply 'I wish I could!' Modern psychology has particular wisdom at this point: I continue to choose such states because I cannot face the truth; I cannot face the feelings of long ago.

We are on holy ground here, for we are sifting the soil out of which we exist and grow, and as Jesus pointed out a long time ago in his parable of the four soils, soil determines everything. History shows that human beings like the idea of wise words. But history also shows that wise words make very little difference to anyone, unless there is good soil for them to grow in, and that soil simply does not exist in the vast majority of human lives. And the reason our soil is as it is, lies in our childhood.

With so little understanding of the origins of behaviour down the years, people have been demonized and punished for their childhood experiences – experiences which left them slaves to attitudes and desires which they had very little control over. Even the beautiful experience of grace can be destroyed by the desperate struggle with early conditioning. How often we see grace flourish for awhile in a life, only then to stagger on the hard rocks of an unexamined past, finally falling, unable to carry on, but not knowing why. It is sometimes called 'loss of faith'; it is sometimes called a nervous breakdown; it is sometimes called a stress-related illness. It is more often simply our unexpressed childhood calling.

The first-century Jesus does not speak the language of twentieth-century psychology - a feature of his life for which many will be thankful. But he lives authentically within its insights, enacting its truths in a most startling manner. He instinctively knew in his body what Freud discovered through his work, understanding that the power of the family must be dismantled before there can be true human flowering. Jesus stands in the shadow of the towering icon which is the family - and pulls it to the ground. He understands that the family must die in order for the individual to live; that the family must die before the family itself can live. Simply to anoint family life as it was - as the moralists would have expected him to do - would merely have been to validate and perpetuate its destructive power. But with the family dead, the freed child could live and return in time as healer.

*

And now a footnote to our true story of Amelia - the girl who thought she had left home at seventeen, but discovered that was not so. In an attempt to understand her feelings on the death of her nan, she had to face things she didn't want to face, things she had sealed from her conscious experience - her difficult relationships with her father and her mother.

When she asked her mother about it, she denied everything. Everything had been fine, she would say. 'I really don't know what you are talking about, Amelia.' Amelia refused to collude in this pretence, and for six months, things were awkward. Amelia struggled to see a way back to any sort of relationship with her mother. In the meantime, she was happy enough in herself, for suddenly everything made sense. She walked the earth as a free person, trusting herself, understanding her reactions to situations better and glimpsing who she might truly be.

The chasm between her and her mother remained until Christmas, when in a phone call, her mother apologized. For the first time, she acknowledged the truth of what Amelia was saying, said she didn't know what to do, but was very sorry. They talked about the past for an hour and a half. Amelia said it was the best Christmas present she had ever had. Things could not go back to how they had been, but then she would not have wanted that, for things had stopped being good a very long time ago.

Things can now go forward, however. In what manner, she does not know, but there is hope. It has been a painful anointing of family. It involved truthful but hard words, and a refusal to collude in bad family pasts and dishonest presents. But it also created shared insight, honesty, apology - and a resurrection of relationships, as in the Gospel story.

*

We have said that life is not complicated. It is difficult, but not complicated, and consisting of two primary movements. The first is the discernment of that which brings life, and the second, the taking of action towards that end. Discernment requires careful listening and maybe painful honesty, while the taking of action requires energy and huge courage. But the inspiration for both discernment and action lies in the glory of encounter - the encounter in time, with that which is outside time; the linear infused by the eternal, in which the beyond is made present, and the present, beyond.

More primary than moralizing religion, is the religion of encounter. Encounter is the ore from which the finest religion is mined. Encounter doesn't preach, for it is not a moral tale - rather, it is the spontaneous transformation of the scenery around you, in a manner which leaves you unable to continue as you are. You may be tethered and tied but you are also looking at the stars. It is a strange and sometimes frightening blessing, a burning bush of heightened moment, awareness and knowing, spilling out from our inmost selves, where it has lain hidden for so long. It is an inner voice of peculiar authority, which takes us beyond the cramped and gloomy corridors of rigid rule and the slavish following of other people's ideas. Instead, the music of possibility breaks out in the sun-lounge of our soul. It is music uniquely our own, entirely personal and brings with it strength for all things.

*

There is a ladder of ascent in the pursuit of understanding and we are not all in the same place. The climb is open to all, but it cannot be hurried, for each step must be lived. There is pleasure to be had in all places, for each step has its own discoveries. On this ladder are the asleep, the awakening and the awakened.

The asleep notice neither pain nor life.

The awakening feel the pain pressing, and experience the struggle of life.

The awakened transcend the pain, allowing it to become a messenger announcing life.

The asleep assume family.

The awakening face family.

The awakened grace family.

*

At the beginning of this book, we asserted that the family has been the single most destructive institution on earth, creating, as it does, so much evil out of so much beauty. It is the family which alienates people from their true selves; it is the family which casts them out into the inner wilderness of their false selves, from which they attempt to live. Such people take out their rage on the world.

And so it is that family - and in particular, the early months and years of nurture - has much to answer for. It is this inadequacy of the early holding environment that is so crucial in the disintegrating process in the human.

Whatever the family arrangement, the human soul of the child is both needy and dependent. If the child's carers are perceived as welcoming, responsive, competent and understanding, then the possibility of a hopeful walk is created in the child - a possibility which will never desert it. But an environment which is perceived as rejecting, neglecting, incompetent or cold will cripple the hopeful walk in profound ways, leaving such residue as fear, frustration, anger and sadness, the terrible offspring of inadequate early holding. The dream and the nightmare of family lie very close together.

In giving John and Mary to each other from the cross, and in seeking out his dear friend Mary Magdalene and his brother James after his rising from death, Jesus anoints the different possibilities of family, and invites us to continue with the dream, even in the face of nightmare.

His life shows family to be a flawed organism, and one with a terrible potential for evil, but one also open to change and adaptation; to healing and to being healed and to the transformation of encounter, amid the chances and changes of this fleeting world.

The family is dead. Long live the family.

Farewells

Each human is a lantern in which burns an eternal flame of strength and beauty. It is not a flame that can be extinguished by anything or anyone.

But it can be covered over and hidden, buried deep in the sand and silt of life. The quality of light given out, therefore, is not dependent on the flame itself, but on the condition of the lantern in which it is set. Sometimes if tilted one way, the silt is dispersed, and the lantern reveals light. But if tilted another way, the light is clogged up with residue and the lantern offers only more darkness.

The silt and the sand in the lantern are acquired from various sources, but the most viscous and enduring is that of childhood. The future for our lantern lies not in increasingly desperate tilting, that we might put the best face on things. Rather, it lies in the removal of the residue of times past, sitting sluggish now within; for though the times may be past, in the deepest places, they are still not forgotten.

We are eager these days to 'draw a line under events', or to 'move on.' But there is no line and no real movement if issues are not faced and dealt with. Eagerness to forget is often nothing more than an ungraced and lazy desire for convenience. The hopeful walk is necessarily a truthful walk, characterized by clear-sighted realism. We cannot forget what we have not first remembered; just as we cannot release what we have not first held and felt. We seek peace, but we should not cry 'Peace!' when there is no peace.

But through and beyond true remembering and feeling, we can indeed cry 'Peace!' When we emerge from the wall of fire, we lie foetus-like in the new surroundings. Dawn has broken and will continue to break daily in the heart of the freed.

*

Truth is strange to our ears because it is so rare; but central to family life is the fact that it does not exist in any very substantial sense. And this is to be considered wholly good news. We might here remember a scene from the life of Jesus when those negative towards him were trying to catch him out over the eternal nature of marriage. They felt they had come up with a conundrum which was going to make Jesus look very foolish. Who would a woman be married to in heaven, they asked, if she had been married to more than one person on earth? Now there was a tricky one for the so-called Teacher to handle!

Jesus is quite under-whelmed by their mean-spirited cleverness. The premise of the conundrum is that relationships on earth will continue as they are beyond the grave, making for hellish chaos, dispute and bad feeling. But Jesus does not accept this premise. He simply replies that things will not be like that; that if we look to the eternal future, we are looking at a different way of being.

Our slightly complex network of relationships will not be polished up a little and then transferred to the halls of heaven; such concepts as marriage and family, which so dominate earthly life, will have no existence. It will be different. We are presented with mystery, certainly, but not a conundrum, and the only ones left looking foolish in this encounter are those too narrowly obsessed with the confines of the present ways and structures. But then who can blame them? That is what they had been taught from their mother's knee. What else could they do but believe it?

We live family life, and life beyond immediate family, a good deal more gracefully and intelligently if we remember the family's lack of ultimate existence.

We confidently said at the beginning of this book that the family is always with us; only now we discover our confidence was misplaced.

The family is not always with us, for it is not with us in the future, and this has consequences for its standing and status in the present. Like the sands of time, our family is slipping through our fingers, for it does not ultimately exist. Yet strangely, in this enforced letting go, comes genuine relationship - for as we say goodbye, we meet people for the first time.

Because our family does not own us, they might come to know us a little; and we, them.

*

We have attempted in this little book better to understand family, and in doing so, better to understand ourselves. We have each listened, as much as we are able, to the tale of a childhood in search of freedom.

It is extraordinarily difficult being human. No other animal on the planet is asked to live as we do with such a gaping chasm between ideal and reality - between the ideals we aspire to, and the realities we achieve; between greatness and the damage done. The asleep will be oblivious to this chasm, but not those who are waking, who will be increasingly conscious of it: of the gap between the glories they sense and the ordinariness of what they experience; between the dreams they harbour and the nightmares they live; between their idealized self and their actual self.

As the old joke has it:

What do you call a Fly with no wings?
A Walk.

There is no mending of this fracture, for the chasm is what it is to be human. At the heart of being human is the incongruity between body and soul, animal and spirit. Two very different entities are asked to work together within us in harmony, but with only occasional success.

The chasm within us is a given. But we will better understand this chasm, if we understand the family in which it was uniquely and particularly formed. We will continue to live with the fracture. But a fracture we understand is not one we need fear, and not one that can ever hurt ourselves or others.

The asleep know nothing of the chasm.

The awakening feel the chasm.

The awakened laugh at the chasm.

And meanwhile, the wingless Walk is happy enough, for nothing is the end of the story, and possibility lives on. Legs are enough for now. I am a walking miracle. And sometimes the sun is gently present; and sometimes new wings grow.

*

And how will we know the coming of the dawn in our lives? We will know the arrival of the dawn by the quality of the light within us.

For much of our time, we live a grey-wash of experience, pressed little lives swamped by immediate concerns, hallucinating fear, worry and turbulence. In such a manner do we stagger unhappily towards our graves, with our music locked away inside, like a music box at the bottom of the sea. But when the dawn breaks for us, we will know the change. The music box is brought to the surface, and discovered still to be working splendidly! And as we lie there in our new state, dazed by the glory of what we are allowed, it will perhaps be the change in our inner light which is most apparent.

In a sense, most important is not what has or has not happened to us in our families, but rather, the quality of light in which we now consider these things in the cathedral vastness of our souls. Some people use a harsh, exposing and relentless light in which to view family affairs; others opt for the cover of dark, throwing a concealing blanket over everything, making all things unspecific and undeclared in the half-light and the shadows. The true dawn, however, brings a light that resembles neither of these. For the true dawn brings a golden light within - a light of honest seeing, clear assessing, deep knowing, gentle holding and hopeful going.

When we can sit with our family, however conceived, in light such as this, then we are true contemplatives, and both healers and the healed in this tragic and magnificent world.

Epilogue

It is dusk and only a little light creeps in through the heavy curtains. His bedroom is small, but you do not need space to die. I am sitting next to him holding his hand. It is a pale hand, thin watery skin and done with doing now.

His breathing is difficult, choppy and erratic and there is sweat on his forehead. It glistens cold in the half-light, a final anointing before death creeps and crawls its chill way across his body. He is speaking. He is sad, but strong. 'I never lived my own life,' he says. 'Never. Not till now. I just pray for the strength to die my own death.'

He smiled weakly. I sensed the comedy of hope in his despair. And suddenly his pale hand is gripping mine, an urgent clinging. It is his body which is speaking, imploring; his brittle bones grasping mine to touch and tell.

'You must live your own life,' he said to me. 'And all else will follow... all else ... that will be good ...'

The grip was no more, loose and lax. He sighed and his erratic breathing ceased. I closed the eyes which no longer sought me out and placed his hands by his side. He was gone from the place where I sat. I stayed still for awhile, pondering, my hand on his.

It is dusk and only a little light creeps in through the heavy curtains. His bedroom is small, but you do not need space to die. I am sitting next to him holding his hand. It is a pale hand, thin watery skin and done with doing now.

His breathing is difficult, choppy and erratic and there is sweat on his forehead. It glistens cold in the half-light, a final anointing before death creeps and crawls its chill way across his body. He is speaking. He is sad, but strong. 'I never lived my own life,' he says. 'Never. Not till now. I just pray for the strength to die my own death.'

He smiled weakly. I sensed the comedy of hope in his despair. And suddenly his pale hand is gripping mine, an urgent clinging. It is his body which is speaking, imploring; his brittle bones grasping mine to touch and tell.

'You must live your own life,' he said to me. 'And all else will follow... all else ... that will be good ...'

The grip was no more, loose and lax. He sighed and his erratic breathing ceased. I closed the eyes which no longer sought me out and placed his hands by his side. He was gone from the place where I sat. I stayed still for awhile, pondering, my hand on his.

I got up and walked across the room to open the curtains. I was surprised by the invasion. Golden sunlight streamed in and bathed me and my departed friend in its blessing.

And that, I suppose, is when this book began.

Paperbacks also available from
White Crow Books

Leo Tolstoy—*My Religion:*
What I Believe
ISBN 978-1-907355-23-3

Leo Tolstoy—*On Life*
ISBN 978-1-907355-91-2

Leo Tolstoy—*Twenty-three Tales*
ISBN 978-1-907355-29-5

Leo Tolstoy—*What is Religion*
and other writings
ISBN 978-1-907355-28-8

Leo Tolstoy—*Work While*
Ye Have the Light
ISBN 978-1-907355-26-4

Leo Tolstoy with Simon Parke—
Conversations with Tolstoy
ISBN 978-1-907355-25-7

Vincent Van Gogh with
Simon Parke—*Conversations*
with Van Gogh
ISBN 978-1-907355-95-0

Howard Williams with an
Introduction by Leo Tolstoy—*The*
Ethics of Diet: An Anthology of
Vegetarian Thought
ISBN 978-1-907355-21-9

Allan Kardec—*The Spirits Book*
ISBN 978-1-907355-98-1

Wolfgang Amadeus Mozart
with Simon Parke—
Conversations with Mozart
ISBN 978-1-907661-38-9

Jesus of Nazareth with
Simon Parke—*Conversations*
with Jesus of Nazareth
ISBN 978-1-907661-41-9

Thomas à Kempis with Simon
Parke—*The Imitation of Christ*
ISBN 978-1-907661-58-7

Emanuel Swedenborg—
Heaven and Hell
ISBN 978-1-907661-55-6

P.D. Ouspensky—*Tertium Organum:*
The Third Canon of Thought
ISBN 978-1-907661-47-1

Dwight Goddard—*A Buddhist Bible*
ISBN 978-1-907661-44-0

Leo Tolstoy—*The Death*
of Ivan Ilyich
ISBN 978-1-907661-10-5

Leo Tolstoy—*Resurrection*
ISBN 978-1-907661-09-9

Michael Tymn—*The Afterlife*
Revealed
ISBN 978-1-970661-90-7

Guy L. Playfair—*If This Be Magic*
ISBN 978-1-907661-84-6

Julian of Norwich with
Simon Parke—*Revelations of*
Divine Love
ISBN 978-1-907661-88-4

Maurice Nicoll—*The New Man*
ISBN 978-1-907661-86-0

Carl Wickland, M.D.—*Thirty Years*
Among the Dead
ISBN 978-1-907661-72-3

Allan Kardec—*The Book on*
Mediums
ISBN 978-1-907661-75-4

John E. Mack—*Passport to the*
Cosmos
ISBN 978-1-907661-81-5

**All titles available as eBooks, and selected titles available in Hardback and
Audiobook formats from www.whitecrowbooks.com**

Lightning Source UK Ltd.
Milton Keynes UK
UKOW051930141111

182047UK00002B/292/P